UNDERSTANDING MACHINE LEARNING
WITH JAVA AND WEKA

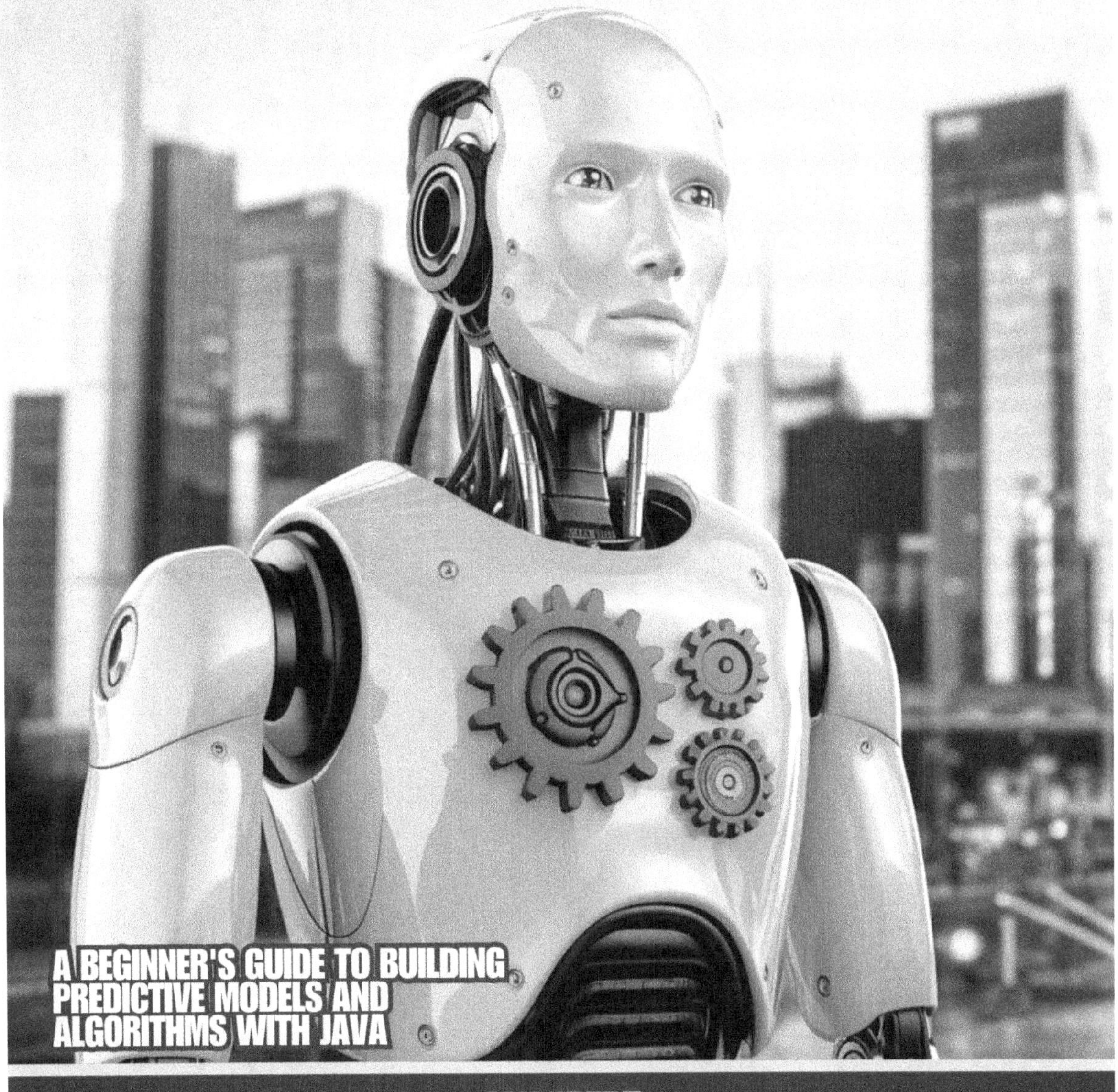

A BEGINNER'S GUIDE TO BUILDING PREDICTIVE MODELS AND ALGORITHMS WITH JAVA

IAN EBERT

COPYRIGHT

© [2024] by Ian Ebert All rights reserved.

No part of this publication may be reproduced, distributed, or transmitted in any form or by any means, including photocopying, recording, or other electronic or mechanical methods, without the prior written permission of the publisher, except in the case of brief quotations embodied in critical reviews and certain other noncommercial uses permitted by copyright law.

Contents

Chapter 1: Introduction to Machine Learning 5
   What is Machine Learning? 5
   Types of Machine Learning: Supervised, Unsupervised, and Reinforcement Learning 5
      Supervised Learning 5
      Unsupervised Learning 6
      Reinforcement Learning 6
   Real-world Applications of Machine Learning 7
      Healthcare 7
      Finance 7
      Marketing 7
      Autonomous Systems 7
      Natural Language Processing 8
   Overview of Java and Weka in Machine Learning 8

Chapter 2: Setting Up Your Development Environment 9
   Installing Java Development Kit (JDK) 9
      Choosing the Right Version 9
      Installation Steps 9
   Setting Up an Integrated Development Environment (IDE) 10
      Popular Java IDEs 10
      Installation Steps 11
      Configuring Your IDE 11
   Downloading and Installing Weka 11
      Installation Steps 11
   Configuring Libraries and Dependencies 12
      Using Build Tools 12
      Best Practices 13

Chapter 3: Understanding Data and Its Importance 15
   Types of Data: Structured vs. Unstructured 15
      Structured Data 15
      Unstructured Data 15
   Data Preprocessing: Cleaning, Normalization, and Transformation 16
      Data Cleaning 16
      Data Normalization 16
      Data Transformation 17
   Introduction to Datasets and Weka's ARFF Format 18
      Common Dataset Formats 18
      Structure of ARFF Files 18

    Benefits of Using ARFF Format in Weka..19
Chapter 4: Exploring Weka: A Comprehensive Overview..**20**
    Introduction to Weka..20
        Key Features of Weka...20
    Installing and Setting Up Weka..21
        Installation Steps..21
        Configuration and Preferences..21
    Weka's GUI Components..22
        Explorer..22
        Knowledge Flow...22
        Experimenter..23
    Working with Datasets in Weka..23
        Importing Datasets...23
        Visualizing Data..23
        Preprocessing Data..24
    Conclusion..24
Chapter 5: Machine Learning Fundamentals..**25**
    Introduction to Machine Learning..25
        Key Concepts in Machine Learning...25
    Types of Machine Learning..25
        Supervised Learning..26
            Key Characteristics...26
            Common Algorithms..26
        Unsupervised Learning..26
            Key Characteristics...26
            Common Algorithms..26
        Reinforcement Learning..27
            Key Characteristics...27
            Common Algorithms..27
    The Machine Learning Workflow...27
        Step 1: Problem Definition..27
        Step 2: Data Collection..27
        Step 3: Data Preprocessing...28
        Step 4: Exploratory Data Analysis (EDA)...28
        Step 5: Model Selection...28
        Step 6: Model Training...28
        Step 7: Model Evaluation...28
        Step 8: Hyperparameter Tuning...28
        Step 9: Deployment...28
    Conclusion..29
Chapter 6: Supervised Learning Algorithms..**30**

- Overview of Supervised Learning...30
  - Key Characteristics of Supervised Learning...30
- Linear Regression...30
  - Introduction..30
  - Mechanics..30
  - Advantages..31
  - Disadvantages...31
  - Applications...31
- Logistic Regression..31
  - Introduction..31
  - Mechanics..31
  - Advantages..32
  - Disadvantages...32
  - Applications...32
- Decision Trees..32
  - Introduction..32
  - Mechanics..32
  - Advantages..33
  - Disadvantages...33
  - Applications...33
- Support Vector Machines (SVM)..33
  - Introduction..33
  - Mechanics..33
  - Advantages..34
  - Disadvantages...34
  - Applications...34
- Neural Networks...34
  - Introduction..34
  - Mechanics..34
  - Advantages..35
  - Disadvantages...35
  - Applications...35
- Conclusion..35

Chapter 7: Unsupervised Learning Algorithms...36
- Overview of Unsupervised Learning..36
  - Key Characteristics of Unsupervised Learning...36
- Clustering Algorithms..36
  - K-Means Clustering...36
    - Introduction..36
    - Mechanics..36
    - Advantages..37

- Disadvantages 37
- Applications 37
- Hierarchical Clustering 37
  - Introduction 37
  - Mechanics 37
  - Advantages 37
  - Disadvantages 38
  - Applications 38
- Dimensionality Reduction Algorithms 38
  - Principal Component Analysis (PCA) 38
    - Introduction 38
    - Mechanics 38
    - Advantages 38
    - Disadvantages 39
    - Applications 39
  - t-Distributed Stochastic Neighbor Embedding (t-SNE) 39
    - Introduction 39
    - Mechanics 39
    - Advantages 39
    - Disadvantages 39
    - Applications 40
- Association Rule Learning 40
  - Apriori Algorithm 40
    - Introduction 40
    - Mechanics 40
    - Advantages 40
    - Disadvantages 40
    - Applications 40
  - FP-Growth Algorithm 41
    - Introduction 41
    - Mechanics 41
    - Advantages 41
    - Disadvantages 41
    - Applications 41
- Conclusion 41

Chapter 8: Model Evaluation and Validation Techniques 42
- Overview of Model Evaluation 42
  - Importance of Model Evaluation 42
- Evaluation Metrics 42
  - Classification Metrics 42
  - Regression Metrics 43

- Cross-Validation Techniques... 43
  - K-Fold Cross-Validation... 44
    - Advantages.. 44
    - Disadvantages.. 44
  - Stratified K-Fold Cross-Validation... 44
  - Leave-One-Out Cross-Validation (LOOCV)... 44
  - Train-Test Split.. 44
- Bias-Variance Tradeoff.. 44
- Best Practices for Model Evaluation.. 45
- Conclusion... 45

Chapter 9: Feature Selection and Dimensionality Reduction........................ 46
- Overview of Feature Selection and Dimensionality Reduction..................... 46
  - Importance of Feature Selection and Dimensionality Reduction............. 46
- Feature Selection Techniques... 46
  - Filter Methods.. 46
    - Advantages of Filter Methods... 47
    - Disadvantages of Filter Methods.. 47
  - Wrapper Methods.. 47
    - Advantages of Wrapper Methods... 47
    - Disadvantages of Wrapper Methods.. 47
  - Embedded Methods.. 47
    - Advantages of Embedded Methods... 48
    - Disadvantages of Embedded Methods.. 48
- Dimensionality Reduction Techniques.. 48
  - Principal Component Analysis (PCA)... 48
    - Advantages of PCA... 48
    - Disadvantages of PCA.. 49
  - t-Distributed Stochastic Neighbor Embedding (t-SNE)............................. 49
    - Advantages of t-SNE... 49
    - Disadvantages of t-SNE.. 49
  - Linear Discriminant Analysis (LDA)... 49
    - Advantages of LDA... 50
    - Disadvantages of LDA.. 50
- Best Practices for Feature Selection and Dimensionality Reduction............ 50
- Conclusion... 50

Chapter 10: Ensemble Learning Methods... 52
- Overview of Ensemble Learning... 52
  - Importance of Ensemble Learning.. 52
- Types of Ensemble Learning Methods... 52
  - Bagging (Bootstrap Aggregating).. 52
    - Key Characteristics... 52

- Common Algorithms.. 53
- Advantages of Bagging.. 53
- Disadvantages of Bagging... 53
- Boosting... 53
  - Key Characteristics... 53
  - Common Algorithms.. 53
  - Advantages of Boosting... 54
  - Disadvantages of Boosting.. 54
- Ensemble Learning Strategies... 54
  - Voting... 54
  - Stacking... 54
    - Key Characteristics... 54
    - Advantages of Stacking... 55
    - Disadvantages of Stacking.. 55
- Practical Applications of Ensemble Learning... 55
- Best Practices for Ensemble Learning.. 55
- Conclusion.. 56

Chapter 11: Neural Networks and Deep Learning with Java................................57
- Overview of Neural Networks and Deep Learning.. 57
  - Importance of Neural Networks and Deep Learning................................. 57
- Fundamentals of Neural Networks... 57
  - Structure of a Neural Network... 57
  - Activation Functions.. 57
  - Forward Propagation.. 58
  - Loss Function... 58
  - Backpropagation.. 58
- Deep Learning Concepts... 59
  - Deep Neural Networks (DNN).. 59
  - Convolutional Neural Networks (CNN)... 59
  - Recurrent Neural Networks (RNN).. 59
  - Transfer Learning... 59
- Implementing Neural Networks in Java... 60
  - Libraries for Neural Networks in Java... 60
  - Building a Neural Network with Deeplearning4j... 60
- Challenges in Neural Network Training.. 61
- Best Practices for Neural Network Development... 62
- Conclusion.. 62

Chapter 12: Model Evaluation and Hyperparameter Tuning................................63
- Overview of Model Evaluation and Hyperparameter Tuning.......................... 63
  - Importance of Model Evaluation... 63
- Model Evaluation Metrics.. 63

  Classification Metrics... 63
  Regression Metrics... 64
 Model Validation Strategies.. 64
  Train-Test Split.. 65
  Cross-Validation.. 65
  Leave-One-Out Cross-Validation (LOOCV).. 65
  Bootstrapping.. 65
 Hyperparameter Tuning.. 65
  Manual Search.. 65
  Grid Search... 66
  Random Search.. 66
  Bayesian Optimization.. 66
  Use of Libraries for Tuning... 66
 Best Practices for Model Evaluation and Tuning... 67
 Conclusion.. 67

Chapter 13: Feature Selection and Engineering..**68**
 Overview of Feature Selection and Engineering... 68
  Importance of Feature Selection and Engineering... 68
 Feature Selection Techniques.. 68
  Filter Methods... 68
  Wrapper Methods... 69
  Embedded Methods... 69
 Feature Engineering Techniques... 69
  Transformation... 69
  Creation of New Features.. 70
  Encoding Categorical Variables... 70
 Implementing Feature Selection and Engineering in Java.. 70
  Using Weka for Feature Selection... 70
  Feature Engineering with Weka... 71
  Example of Creating Interaction Features.. 71
 Best Practices for Feature Selection and Engineering... 72
 Conclusion.. 72

Chapter 14: Ensemble Learning Techniques...**73**
 Overview of Ensemble Learning Techniques.. 73
  Importance of Ensemble Learning.. 73
 Types of Ensemble Learning Methods... 73
  Bagging (Bootstrap Aggregating)... 73
   Random Forest... 74
  Boosting.. 74
   AdaBoost... 74
   Gradient Boosting... 75

    Implementing Ensemble Learning in Java with Weka... 75
        Using Random Forest in Weka.. 75
        Using AdaBoost in Weka.. 76
        Using Gradient Boosting in Weka.. 76
    Best Practices for Ensemble Learning... 77
    Conclusion.. 77

Chapter 15: Model Deployment and Maintenance..78
    Overview of Model Deployment and Maintenance.. 78
        Importance of Model Deployment... 78
    Steps in Model Deployment... 78
        1. Model Serialization... 78
        2. Setting Up the Production Environment.. 79
        3. Model Integration.. 79
        4. Testing in Production... 79
    Challenges in Model Deployment... 80
        1. Data Drift... 80
        2. Model Versioning.. 80
        3. Scalability... 80
        4. Security Concerns.. 80
    Model Maintenance Strategies.. 80
        1. Regular Monitoring and Evaluation... 80
        2. Periodic Retraining... 81
        3. Automated Monitoring Systems.. 81
        4. Model Explainability.. 81
    Best Practices for Model Deployment and Maintenance... 81
    Conclusion.. 82

Chapter 16: Ethical Considerations in Machine Learning...83
    Overview of Ethical Considerations in Machine Learning.. 83
        Importance of Ethical Considerations... 83
    Key Ethical Issues in Machine Learning.. 83
        1. Bias and Fairness.. 83
        2. Transparency and Explainability... 84
        3. Privacy and Data Protection.. 84
        4. Accountability and Responsibility.. 84
        5. Societal Impact.. 85
    Frameworks for Ethical Decision-Making.. 85
        1. The Fairness Framework.. 85
        2. The Accountability Framework... 85
        3. The Transparency Framework.. 85
        4. The Ethical Review Framework... 86
    Strategies for Implementing Ethical Practices.. 86

- 1. Conduct Ethical Assessments.. 86
- 2. Promote Diversity in Teams.. 86
- 3. Invest in Education and Training... 86
- 4. Engage with the Community... 86
- 5. Establish Ethical Guidelines.. 87
- Conclusion.. 87

Chapter 17: Future Trends in Machine Learning... 88
- Overview of Future Trends in Machine Learning.. 88
  - Importance of Staying Ahead of Trends.. 88
- Emerging Trends in Machine Learning.. 88
  - 1. Automated Machine Learning (AutoML)... 88
  - 2. Explainable AI (XAI).. 89
  - 3. Federated Learning... 89
  - 4. Ethical AI and Governance.. 89
  - 5. Integration of AI and IoT... 90
  - 6. Edge Computing and On-Device Learning... 90
  - 7. Enhanced Natural Language Processing (NLP)....................................... 90
  - 8. Advanced Reinforcement Learning... 90
- Conclusion.. 91

Chapter 1: Introduction to Machine Learning

What is Machine Learning?

Machine Learning (ML) is a subset of artificial intelligence (AI) that focuses on the development of algorithms and statistical models that enable computers to perform specific tasks without explicit instructions. Instead of programming specific rules, ML systems learn from data and improve their performance over time. This capability allows machines to identify patterns, make decisions, and predict outcomes based on past experiences.

At its core, machine learning revolves around the idea of creating models that can generalize from observed data to unseen situations. For instance, consider a model trained on images of cats and dogs. Once trained, the model can classify new images as either a cat or a dog based on the features it learned during training. This ability to generalize is crucial for many applications, as it enables systems to adapt to new data, which is common in real-world scenarios.

The importance of machine learning has grown exponentially in recent years, driven by the explosion of data generated across various sectors. The increasing availability of large datasets, combined with advancements in computing power, has facilitated the development of more sophisticated algorithms that can analyze and derive insights from this data. Consequently, machine learning is now integral to diverse fields, including finance, healthcare, marketing, and autonomous systems.

Types of Machine Learning: Supervised, Unsupervised, and Reinforcement Learning

Machine learning can be broadly categorized into three main types: supervised learning, unsupervised learning, and reinforcement learning. Each type has distinct characteristics, methodologies, and applications.

Supervised Learning

Supervised learning is the most common type of machine learning, where a model is trained on a labeled dataset. In this context, "labeled" means that each training example is paired with an output label or target value. The objective is to learn a mapping from inputs to outputs that can then be applied to new, unseen data.

For example, in a supervised learning scenario involving email classification, the model might be trained on a dataset of emails labeled as "spam" or "not spam." The algorithm learns to recognize patterns in the data that correlate with each label, allowing it to classify new emails accurately. Common supervised learning algorithms include linear regression, logistic regression, decision trees, support vector machines, and neural networks.

Supervised learning is particularly effective when historical data is available, and the relationships between features and outputs can be well defined. It is widely used in applications such as fraud detection, image recognition, and natural language processing.

Unsupervised Learning

In contrast to supervised learning, unsupervised learning deals with datasets that do not have labeled outputs. Instead of predicting a specific outcome, the goal is to explore the underlying structure or distribution of the data. This type of learning is particularly useful for discovering patterns, groupings, or anomalies within datasets.

Clustering is a primary technique used in unsupervised learning, where the algorithm groups similar data points based on their features. For example, in customer segmentation, an unsupervised learning algorithm might analyze purchasing behavior data to identify distinct customer segments without prior knowledge of the groups. Other techniques include dimensionality reduction methods, such as Principal Component Analysis (PCA), which reduce the number of features while preserving as much information as possible.

Unsupervised learning is widely used in applications like market research, recommendation systems, and anomaly detection. Its ability to uncover hidden patterns makes it a powerful tool for exploratory data analysis.

Reinforcement Learning

Reinforcement learning (RL) is a unique approach that focuses on training agents to make decisions through trial and error. In RL, an agent interacts with an environment and learns to take actions that maximize cumulative rewards. This learning paradigm is inspired by behavioral psychology, where learning occurs through rewards and punishments.

In a reinforcement learning scenario, the agent receives feedback in the form of rewards or penalties based on its actions. For instance, in a game-playing environment, the agent might earn points for winning a level and lose points for making poor moves. Over time, the agent learns to optimize its strategy to achieve the highest possible score.

Reinforcement learning is particularly effective in complex environments where traditional supervised or unsupervised learning may struggle. Applications include robotics, game playing (like AlphaGo), and autonomous vehicles. The ability to learn from interactions with an environment makes RL a powerful tool for tasks that require decision-making under uncertainty.

Real-world Applications of Machine Learning

Machine learning has transformed various industries by providing innovative solutions to complex problems. Below are some notable applications across different fields:

Healthcare

In healthcare, machine learning is used to improve patient outcomes, streamline operations, and enhance diagnostic accuracy. Algorithms analyze medical images, such as X-rays or MRIs, to assist radiologists in detecting anomalies like tumors. Predictive analytics in healthcare can forecast disease outbreaks, identify patients at risk for specific conditions, and optimize treatment plans based on individual patient data.

Finance

The finance industry leverages machine learning for tasks such as credit scoring, fraud detection, and algorithmic trading. By analyzing historical transaction data, ML models can identify patterns indicative of fraudulent activity, enabling banks to act swiftly. In investment, ML algorithms predict stock prices by analyzing market trends and historical performance, providing valuable insights for traders.

Marketing

In marketing, machine learning enhances customer engagement and personalization. Algorithms analyze customer behavior and preferences, allowing businesses to tailor their marketing strategies effectively. Recommendation systems, such as those used by Netflix and Amazon, leverage machine learning to suggest products or content based on user interactions, significantly improving user experience and sales conversion rates.

Autonomous Systems

Machine learning plays a pivotal role in the development of autonomous systems, including self-driving cars and drones. These systems rely on ML algorithms to process sensor data, recognize objects, and make real-time decisions in dynamic environments. The integration of computer vision and reinforcement learning enables these vehicles to navigate complex road conditions safely.

Natural Language Processing

Natural language processing (NLP) applications, powered by machine learning, allow computers to understand, interpret, and generate human language. From chatbots providing customer support to sentiment analysis tools that gauge public opinion, NLP technologies rely on ML to analyze text data and derive insights, transforming the way businesses interact with their customers.

Overview of Java and Weka in Machine Learning

Java is a versatile, object-oriented programming language widely used in enterprise applications, making it an ideal choice for developing machine learning algorithms. Its platform independence, extensive libraries, and robust community support contribute to its popularity among developers and researchers.

Weka, short for Waikato Environment for Knowledge Analysis, is a powerful open-source software suite for machine learning and data mining tasks. Developed in Java, Weka provides a collection of machine learning algorithms and tools for data preprocessing, classification, regression, clustering, and visualization. Its user-friendly interface and comprehensive documentation make it accessible for beginners and experts alike.

Weka's versatility allows users to apply machine learning techniques to various datasets seamlessly. The ability to visualize data and model performance enhances the understanding of underlying patterns and results. Additionally, Weka's integration with Java allows developers to build custom machine learning applications, leveraging the full power of both the language and the toolkit.

In summary, machine learning represents a paradigm shift in how we approach data analysis and decision-making. By understanding the core concepts, types, and applications of machine learning, along with the role of Java and Weka, readers will be well-equipped to embark on their journey into the world of predictive analytics and data modeling. As we delve deeper into the chapters that follow, the practical implementation of these concepts will become increasingly clear, empowering readers to harness the potential of machine learning in their projects.

Chapter 2: Setting Up Your Development Environment

Installing Java Development Kit (JDK)

To begin your journey into machine learning with Java and Weka, the first step is to install the Java Development Kit (JDK). The JDK is essential as it provides the tools needed to develop Java applications, including the Java Runtime Environment (JRE), compiler, and various utilities.

Choosing the Right Version

When installing the JDK, it's crucial to choose the right version. As of my last knowledge update, Java 8 and Java 11 are the most widely used versions in enterprise applications, although newer versions like Java 17 have also gained popularity. While it's often beneficial to use the latest stable version for new features and enhancements, ensure that any libraries or frameworks you plan to use are compatible with the chosen version.

Installation Steps

1. **Download the JDK**: Visit the official Oracle website or adopt OpenJDK, an open-source implementation. Select the version appropriate for your operating system (Windows, macOS, or Linux).
2. **Install the JDK**:
    - **Windows**: Run the downloaded installer and follow the prompts. During installation, you may choose to set the installation directory or use the default location.
    - **macOS**: Open the downloaded .dmg file and follow the instructions to install. The JDK will typically be installed in the `/Library/Java/JavaVirtualMachines/` directory.

Linux: You can use package managers like `apt` for Debian-based systems or `yum` for Red Hat-based systems. For example, to install OpenJDK on Ubuntu, you would use:
bash
Copy code
```
sudo apt update
sudo apt install openjdk-11-jdk
```

-
   3. **Set Environment Variables**:
      - **Windows**: After installation, you need to set the `JAVA_HOME` environment variable to point to the JDK installation directory. Go to Control Panel > System and Security > System > Advanced System Settings > Environment Variables. Under System Variables, click New and add `JAVA_HOME` with the path to your JDK.

macOS/Linux: You can set `JAVA_HOME` in your shell configuration file (e.g., `.bashrc`, `.bash_profile`, or `.zshrc`):

bash
Copy code
```
export JAVA_HOME=/Library/Java/JavaVirtualMachines/jdk-11.jdk/Contents/Home
export PATH=$JAVA_HOME/bin:$PATH
```

   -

Verify the Installation: Open a terminal or command prompt and type:
bash
Copy code
```
java -version
```

   4. This command should display the installed version of Java, confirming that the installation was successful.

Setting Up an Integrated Development Environment (IDE)

While you can write Java code in a simple text editor, using an Integrated Development Environment (IDE) significantly enhances productivity. An IDE provides features like code completion, debugging tools, and project management capabilities that streamline the development process.

Popular Java IDEs

1. **Eclipse**: A widely used open-source IDE for Java development. It offers a robust plugin ecosystem, making it suitable for various programming tasks, including machine learning.

2. **IntelliJ IDEA**: Known for its intelligent code assistance, IntelliJ IDEA is another popular choice among developers. It has both a free Community Edition and a paid Ultimate Edition, offering additional features.
3. **NetBeans**: This IDE is user-friendly and integrates well with JavaFX for graphical applications. It is also open-source and provides a rich set of tools for Java developers.

Installation Steps

- **Eclipse**:
    1. Download the Eclipse IDE from the official website.
    2. Extract the downloaded file and run the `eclipse` executable.
    3. Select a workspace directory where your projects will be stored.
- **IntelliJ IDEA**:
    1. Download IntelliJ IDEA from the JetBrains website.
    2. Run the installer and follow the prompts.
    3. Choose the installation options that suit your needs, including plugins and themes.
- **NetBeans**:
    1. Download the NetBeans installer from the Apache NetBeans website.
    2. Run the installer and follow the installation instructions.

Configuring Your IDE

After installing an IDE, it's important to configure it for optimal performance:

- **Set the JDK**: Ensure your IDE is configured to use the installed JDK. This is typically done in the IDE settings under the "Project Structure" or "Preferences" menu.
- **Install Necessary Plugins**: Depending on your needs, you may want to install plugins that enhance functionality, such as version control (Git), formatting tools, or additional machine learning libraries.

Downloading and Installing Weka

Weka is a powerful and user-friendly tool for machine learning that simplifies the process of data analysis and model building. Installing Weka is straightforward and can be done on multiple platforms.

Installation Steps

1. **Download Weka**: Visit the official Weka website, where you can find the latest version available for download. The software is available as a standalone application, or you can download the source code if you wish to compile it yourself.
2. **Install Weka**:
    - **Windows**: Run the downloaded installer, which will guide you through the installation process. By default, Weka will be installed in the `C:\Program Files\Weka-<version>` directory.
    - **macOS**: Open the downloaded `.dmg` file and drag the Weka application to the Applications folder.

Linux: You can download the `.tar.gz` file and extract it to a directory of your choice. To run Weka, navigate to the directory in a terminal and execute:
bash
Copy code
```
java -jar weka.jar
```

   -
3. **Verify Weka Installation**: After installation, you can verify it by launching the application. You should see Weka's GUI, which offers various tools for data processing, modeling, and evaluation.

Configuring Libraries and Dependencies

For effective machine learning development, it's crucial to manage your project's libraries and dependencies. Many machine learning tasks require specific libraries to function correctly, and managing these dependencies ensures that your application runs smoothly.

Using Build Tools

To streamline dependency management in Java projects, consider using build automation tools like Maven or Gradle. These tools allow you to define your project's dependencies in a structured format, and they automatically handle downloading and updating these libraries.

1. **Maven**:
    - Create a `pom.xml` file in your project root directory. This file contains information about your project and its dependencies.

Add Weka as a dependency in the `pom.xml` file:
xml
Copy code
```xml
<dependency>
    <groupId>nz.ac.waikato.cms.weka</groupId>
    <artifactId>weka-stable</artifactId>
    <version>3.8.5</version>
</dependency>
```

-
2. **Gradle**:
    - Create a `build.gradle` file in your project directory. This file defines your project's configuration and dependencies.

Add the Weka dependency:
groovy
Copy code
```groovy
dependencies {
    implementation 'nz.ac.waikato.cms.weka:weka-stable:3.8.5'
}
```

-

Using these build tools not only simplifies dependency management but also enhances collaboration, as other developers can easily replicate the environment by running a single command.

Best Practices

- **Keep Dependencies Updated**: Regularly check for updates to your libraries to benefit from new features and security patches.
- **Use Version Control**: Incorporate version control systems like Git into your workflow to manage changes and collaborate with other developers effectively.
- **Document Your Setup**: Create documentation that outlines the setup process for your environment, including installation steps and configuration settings. This documentation will be invaluable for onboarding new team members or revisiting the project later.

In conclusion, setting up your development environment is a critical step in your journey into machine learning with Java and Weka. By installing the JDK, configuring an IDE, downloading Weka, and managing libraries and dependencies, you will lay a solid foundation for exploring and implementing machine learning algorithms. As you progress, this environment will serve as your playground for experimentation and discovery, enabling you to harness the full potential of machine learning in your projects.

Chapter 3: Understanding Data and Its Importance

Types of Data: Structured vs. Unstructured

Data is the cornerstone of machine learning; understanding its types and characteristics is essential for effective analysis and model building. Data can be broadly categorized into structured and unstructured formats, each requiring different handling techniques.

Structured Data

Structured data refers to information that is highly organized and easily searchable within fixed fields or formats. This type of data is typically stored in relational databases or spreadsheets, where each record is represented as a row, and each attribute as a column. The rigidity of structured data makes it ideal for traditional data analysis techniques.

Examples of structured data include:

- **Tabular Data**: Data organized in rows and columns, such as sales records, customer information, or product inventories.
- **Databases**: Data stored in SQL databases, where tables are used to organize information in a defined schema.
- **Data Types**: Structured data is often numerical or categorical, allowing for easy aggregation and statistical analysis.

Structured data is advantageous for machine learning tasks because it allows for straightforward preprocessing and transformation. Many machine learning algorithms, especially those designed for classification and regression, perform well on structured datasets due to their predictable nature.

Unstructured Data

Unstructured data, on the other hand, lacks a predefined format or structure, making it more challenging to analyze and process. This type of data can come in various forms, including text, images, audio, and video. As the volume of unstructured data continues to grow, so does the need for sophisticated techniques to extract meaningful insights.

Examples of unstructured data include:

- **Text Data**: Documents, emails, social media posts, and reviews that require natural language processing (NLP) to analyze sentiment, extract entities, and understand context.
- **Image Data**: Photographs, medical images, and videos that require computer vision techniques for tasks such as object detection, image classification, and segmentation.
- **Audio Data**: Speech recordings, music, and other sound files that can be analyzed using techniques like speech recognition or audio classification.

The challenges posed by unstructured data often necessitate the use of advanced machine learning techniques, such as deep learning, which can effectively handle complex patterns and representations.

Data Preprocessing: Cleaning, Normalization, and Transformation

Data preprocessing is a crucial step in the machine learning pipeline. It involves preparing raw data for analysis by addressing issues like noise, missing values, and inconsistencies. Proper data preprocessing improves model performance and ensures that the algorithms can learn effectively from the input data.

Data Cleaning

Data cleaning focuses on identifying and correcting errors or inconsistencies in the dataset. Common issues include:

- **Missing Values**: Incomplete records can lead to biased or inaccurate models. Depending on the context, missing values can be handled by removing records, imputing values based on statistical techniques (mean, median, mode), or using algorithms that support missing data.
- **Outliers**: Outliers are data points that deviate significantly from the rest of the data. They can skew results and lead to misleading conclusions. Techniques like z-score analysis or IQR (Interquartile Range) can help identify and manage outliers by either removing them or transforming them.
- **Duplicate Records**: Duplicate entries can arise from data collection processes and can distort analysis. Identifying and removing duplicates is essential to maintain the integrity of the dataset.

Data Normalization

Normalization is the process of scaling numerical features to a standard range, making it easier for algorithms to learn. Different machine learning models have varying sensitivities to feature scales, making normalization a critical step, especially for distance-based algorithms like k-Nearest Neighbors (k-NN) and Support Vector Machines (SVM).

Common normalization techniques include:

- **Min-Max Scaling**: This method scales features to a fixed range, usually [0, 1]. The formula for min-max scaling is:
  $$X_{\text{scaled}} = \frac{X - X_{\text{min}}}{X_{\text{max}} - X_{\text{min}}}$$
- **Z-score Standardization**: This technique transforms features to have a mean of 0 and a standard deviation of 1. The formula is:
  $$X_{\text{standardized}} = \frac{X - \mu}{\sigma}$$
  where μ is the mean and σ is the standard deviation.

Normalization helps ensure that no single feature disproportionately influences the model due to its scale, allowing for better convergence during the training process.

Data Transformation

Data transformation involves changing the format, structure, or values of the data to make it suitable for analysis. This step can include:

- **Encoding Categorical Variables**: Many machine learning algorithms require numerical input. Categorical variables must be converted into a numerical format using techniques like one-hot encoding or label encoding.
- **Feature Engineering**: This involves creating new features from existing ones to enhance model performance. Techniques can include polynomial feature expansion, interaction terms, or aggregating information over time.
- **Dimensionality Reduction**: Reducing the number of features while preserving as much information as possible can enhance model performance and reduce overfitting. Techniques like Principal Component Analysis (PCA) and t-distributed Stochastic Neighbor Embedding (t-SNE) are commonly used for dimensionality reduction.

Effective data preprocessing sets the foundation for successful machine learning models, improving their accuracy and interpretability.

Introduction to Datasets and Weka's ARFF Format

Datasets play a critical role in machine learning, as they provide the necessary information for training and evaluating models. Understanding how to structure and utilize datasets effectively is essential for successful machine learning projects.

Common Dataset Formats

While datasets can come in various formats (CSV, Excel, SQL databases), the ARFF (Attribute-Relation File Format) is particularly important when working with Weka. ARFF files are plain text files that describe instances (data points) and their attributes (features) in a structured manner.

Structure of ARFF Files

An ARFF file consists of two main sections: the header and the data section. The header contains metadata about the dataset, while the data section contains the actual instances.

1. **Header Section**: This section includes information about the dataset, such as:
   - **@RELATION**: Specifies the name of the dataset.
   - **@ATTRIBUTE**: Defines each attribute (feature) along with its data type. Common data types include numeric, nominal, string, and date.

Example header:
less
Copy code
```
@RELATION iris
@ATTRIBUTE sepal_length NUMERIC
@ATTRIBUTE sepal_width NUMERIC
@ATTRIBUTE petal_length NUMERIC
@ATTRIBUTE petal_width NUMERIC
@ATTRIBUTE class {Iris-setosa, Iris-versicolor, Iris-virginica}
```

2.

Data Section: This section starts with the `@DATA` keyword, followed by a list of instances, each represented by a comma-separated set of values. The order of values must correspond to the order of attributes defined in the header.
Example data section:
css

Copy code
```
@DATA
5.1,3.5,1.4,0.2,Iris-setosa
4.9,3.0,1.4,0.2,Iris-setosa
7.0,3.2,4.7,1.4,Iris-versicolor
6.3,3.3,6.0,2.5,Iris-virginica
```

3.

Benefits of Using ARFF Format in Weka

Using the ARFF format in Weka offers several advantages:

- **Simplicity**: The text-based format is easy to read and write, making it accessible for users. You can create or modify ARFF files using any text editor.
- **Integration with Weka**: Weka natively supports ARFF files, making it seamless to import datasets for analysis. You can load, manipulate, and visualize data directly within the Weka GUI.
- **Flexibility**: The ARFF format can accommodate various data types, allowing for diverse datasets to be represented effectively.

In summary, understanding the types of data, the importance of data preprocessing, and the structure of datasets is essential for any machine learning practitioner. As we continue our journey into machine learning with Java and Weka, mastering these concepts will empower you to handle data effectively, ensuring that your models are built on a solid foundation. The ability to clean, normalize, and transform data will set you apart as you delve deeper into the fascinating world of predictive analytics.

Chapter 4: Exploring Weka: A Comprehensive Overview

Introduction to Weka

Weka, short for Waikato Environment for Knowledge Analysis, is an open-source suite of machine learning software written in Java. Developed at the University of Waikato, Weka provides a collection of algorithms and tools for data mining, machine learning, and predictive analytics. It is widely used for academic research, practical applications, and teaching due to its user-friendly interface and powerful capabilities.

Weka's modular architecture allows users to easily integrate various machine learning algorithms and preprocessors. The platform supports numerous data formats, including its native ARFF format, CSV, and others. By providing an extensive set of built-in algorithms and utilities, Weka simplifies the implementation of complex machine learning tasks, making it an ideal choice for beginners and experts alike.

Key Features of Weka

Weka offers several features that enhance its usability and functionality:

- **User-Friendly Interface**: Weka provides a graphical user interface (GUI) that allows users to interact with datasets, apply algorithms, and visualize results without needing extensive programming skills.
- **Extensive Library of Algorithms**: Weka includes a wide range of machine learning algorithms for classification, regression, clustering, and association rule mining. This variety enables users to experiment with different techniques and select the best one for their specific tasks.
- **Data Preprocessing Tools**: Weka comes equipped with various data preprocessing options, including filtering, normalization, and attribute selection. These tools facilitate effective data preparation, ensuring that users can clean and format their datasets before analysis.
- **Visualization Capabilities**: Weka offers several visualization tools that allow users to explore data distributions, relationships between attributes, and the performance of models. Visualizing data can provide insights that guide model selection and refinement.
- **Scripting and Integration**: For users with programming experience, Weka provides an API that allows for automation and integration with Java applications.

This feature enables more advanced users to customize their workflows and create complex models.

Installing and Setting Up Weka

To harness the power of Weka, you need to install and configure the software on your system. The installation process is straightforward and can be completed in a few steps.

Installation Steps

1. **Download Weka**: Visit the official Weka website and download the latest stable version of the software. You will typically find the installer for your operating system (Windows, macOS, or Linux).
2. **Install Weka**:
    - **Windows**: Run the downloaded installer and follow the prompts to complete the installation. By default, Weka will be installed in the `C:\Program Files\Weka-<version>` directory.
    - **macOS**: Open the downloaded `.dmg` file and drag the Weka application into the Applications folder.

Linux: Download the `.tar.gz` file and extract it to a directory of your choice. You can run Weka by navigating to that directory in a terminal and executing:
bash
Copy code
```
java -jar weka.jar
```

   -
3. **Launch Weka**: Once installed, you can launch Weka by executing the application from your system's application menu or terminal.

Configuration and Preferences

After launching Weka, you may want to configure its preferences to optimize your experience:

- **Set Memory Options**: In the preferences, you can adjust the maximum memory allocation for Weka to enhance performance, especially when working with large datasets. This can be done by modifying the Java Virtual Machine (JVM) settings.

- **Choose File Formats**: Weka supports various file formats. Ensure that the default format for importing datasets matches your needs, whether ARFF, CSV, or others.
- **Configure Visualization Options**: Adjust the visualization preferences to enhance the graphical outputs, such as changing colors or display settings, making it easier to interpret data insights.

Weka's GUI Components

Weka's graphical user interface consists of several components that facilitate data analysis and model development. Understanding these components is essential for navigating the software effectively.

Explorer

The Explorer is the primary interface for data analysis in Weka. It allows users to load datasets, preprocess data, apply machine learning algorithms, and visualize results. The Explorer is divided into several tabs:

- **Preprocess Tab**: This section is where you can load datasets, apply filters, and preprocess data. It provides options for removing attributes, handling missing values, and normalizing data.
- **Classify Tab**: In this tab, users can choose from various classification algorithms, set parameters, and evaluate model performance. It allows for training and testing models using cross-validation or a separate test set.
- **Cluster Tab**: This section enables users to apply clustering algorithms to group similar instances within the dataset. You can visualize the clusters and evaluate their characteristics.
- **Associate Tab**: The Associate tab allows for discovering association rules within the dataset. It provides tools for analyzing relationships between attributes and generating rules based on itemsets.
- **Evaluate Tab**: Users can compare and evaluate the performance of multiple models in this tab, allowing for comprehensive analysis of different algorithms.

Knowledge Flow

Weka also offers a Knowledge Flow interface, which allows users to create a data mining workflow visually. Users can drag and drop components representing various tasks (e.g., data loading, preprocessing, modeling) and connect them to create a seamless data analysis pipeline. This feature is particularly useful for more complex analyses requiring multiple steps and transformations.

Experimenter

The Experimenter component in Weka is designed for conducting experiments to evaluate and compare different machine learning algorithms. Users can set up multiple experiments, specify datasets, and define the parameters for each model. The Experimenter automates the evaluation process and provides statistical analysis of the results, making it easier to identify the most effective algorithms for a given problem.

Working with Datasets in Weka

Once Weka is installed and set up, you can begin working with datasets. Understanding how to import, visualize, and preprocess data within Weka is crucial for successful machine learning projects.

Importing Datasets

Weka supports several methods for importing datasets:

- **ARFF Files**: The most common format for Weka, ARFF files can be loaded directly using the Preprocess tab. Simply select "Open file" and choose your ARFF file.
- **CSV Files**: Weka can also import CSV files. When loading CSV files, ensure that the first row contains the attribute names, and that the data is well-formatted to avoid errors during import.
- **Other Formats**: Weka supports other formats such as C4.5 and libSVM, allowing for flexibility in handling datasets.

Visualizing Data

Once your dataset is loaded, Weka offers various visualization tools to explore the data:

- **Attribute Visualization**: Use the "Visualize" panel in the Preprocess tab to create scatter plots and histograms for individual attributes. This visualization helps identify distributions, correlations, and potential outliers.
- **Class Distribution**: Visualize class distributions to understand how the target variable is represented in the dataset. This information is vital for assessing class balance, which can influence model performance.
- **Pairwise Scatter Plots**: Weka allows for the creation of pairwise scatter plots to visualize relationships between attributes. These plots can reveal correlations that inform feature selection and engineering.

Preprocessing Data

Preprocessing data is essential for preparing your dataset for machine learning algorithms. Weka provides a range of preprocessing options:

- **Attribute Selection**: Use filters to select relevant attributes, removing irrelevant or redundant features. Techniques such as correlation-based feature selection can enhance model performance.
- **Data Filtering**: Weka offers several filters for cleaning data, including options for removing missing values, normalizing data, and transforming categorical attributes into numerical ones.
- **Resampling**: If your dataset is imbalanced, Weka provides options for resampling to create balanced training sets, such as oversampling minority classes or undersampling majority classes.

Conclusion

Weka is a powerful tool for machine learning, offering an extensive array of features and functionalities that cater to both beginners and experienced practitioners. By understanding Weka's components, installing and configuring the software, and mastering the manipulation of datasets, users can efficiently implement machine learning algorithms to derive insights from data.

As we progress through the chapters, the knowledge gained about Weka's capabilities will be instrumental in exploring specific algorithms and practical applications in machine learning. This foundation will empower you to tackle real-world problems with confidence, leveraging the full potential of Weka in your projects.

Chapter 5: Machine Learning Fundamentals

Introduction to Machine Learning

Machine learning is a branch of artificial intelligence that focuses on developing algorithms capable of learning from and making predictions based on data. Unlike traditional programming, where explicit rules and logic are coded, machine learning algorithms improve their performance as they are exposed to more data. This ability to learn and adapt is what makes machine learning a powerful tool across various applications, from image recognition and natural language processing to financial forecasting and healthcare diagnostics.

Key Concepts in Machine Learning

1. **Training and Testing**: In machine learning, the dataset is typically divided into two subsets: the training set and the test set. The training set is used to train the model, while the test set evaluates its performance. This division is crucial for assessing the model's ability to generalize to unseen data.
2. **Features and Labels**: Features are the input variables used by the model to make predictions, while labels are the output variables that the model aims to predict. For instance, in a house price prediction model, features may include square footage, location, and number of bedrooms, while the label is the house price.
3. **Overfitting and Underfitting**: Overfitting occurs when a model learns noise and details from the training data to the extent that it negatively impacts its performance on new data. Conversely, underfitting happens when a model is too simple to capture the underlying patterns in the data, leading to poor performance on both training and test sets. Striking a balance between these two extremes is essential for effective model performance.
4. **Evaluation Metrics**: Assessing model performance involves various metrics, depending on the type of problem being solved. Common metrics for classification tasks include accuracy, precision, recall, and F1-score, while regression tasks typically use metrics like mean squared error (MSE) and R-squared.

Types of Machine Learning

Machine learning can be categorized into three primary types: supervised learning, unsupervised learning, and reinforcement learning. Each type has distinct characteristics and applications.

Supervised Learning

In supervised learning, the algorithm is trained on labeled data, where the input features are paired with their corresponding output labels. The goal is for the model to learn the mapping from inputs to outputs and make predictions on unseen data.

Key Characteristics

- **Labeled Data**: Supervised learning requires a dataset with known output labels for training.
- **Direct Feedback**: The model receives feedback on its predictions, allowing it to learn from mistakes and improve over time.

Common Algorithms

- **Linear Regression**: Used for predicting continuous values based on linear relationships between features.
- **Logistic Regression**: Used for binary classification tasks where the output is categorical.
- **Decision Trees**: A tree-like model that splits data into branches to make predictions based on feature values.
- **Support Vector Machines (SVM)**: A powerful algorithm that finds the hyperplane that best separates data into different classes.
- **Neural Networks**: Inspired by the human brain, neural networks consist of interconnected nodes that process data in layers, making them suitable for complex tasks.

Unsupervised Learning

Unsupervised learning deals with datasets that do not contain labeled output variables. The algorithm tries to identify patterns or groupings within the data without explicit guidance.

Key Characteristics

- **No Labeled Data**: Unsupervised learning algorithms work with input data only, discovering hidden structures or relationships.
- **Exploratory Nature**: These algorithms are often used for data exploration and understanding, rather than making predictions.

Common Algorithms

- **K-Means Clustering**: A popular clustering algorithm that partitions data into kkk distinct clusters based on feature similarity.
- **Hierarchical Clustering**: Builds a tree-like structure to represent data hierarchically, useful for understanding data relationships.
- **Principal Component Analysis (PCA)**: A dimensionality reduction technique that transforms data into a lower-dimensional space while preserving variance.

Reinforcement Learning

Reinforcement learning is a unique paradigm where an agent learns to make decisions by interacting with an environment. The agent receives rewards or penalties based on its actions, guiding it to maximize cumulative rewards over time.

Key Characteristics

- **Trial and Error**: The agent explores the environment, learning from successes and failures.
- **Delayed Feedback**: Unlike supervised learning, feedback may not be immediate, requiring the agent to learn from long-term consequences.

Common Algorithms

- **Q-Learning**: A model-free algorithm that learns the value of actions in a given state, aiming to maximize long-term rewards.
- **Deep Q-Networks (DQN)**: Combines reinforcement learning with deep learning, enabling the agent to learn from high-dimensional sensory inputs like images.
- **Policy Gradients**: Directly optimize the policy (the agent's behavior) to improve performance in complex environments.

The Machine Learning Workflow

The process of building machine learning models involves several key steps, often referred to as the machine learning workflow. Understanding this workflow is essential for developing effective machine learning applications.

Step 1: Problem Definition

Clearly define the problem you want to solve. This includes understanding the objectives, constraints, and success criteria. Whether it's classifying emails as spam or predicting stock prices, a well-defined problem sets the foundation for the entire project.

Step 2: Data Collection

Gather relevant data for your problem. This data can come from various sources, including databases, APIs, web scraping, or public datasets. Ensure that the data collected is representative of the problem space.

Step 3: Data Preprocessing

Prepare the data for analysis by cleaning, normalizing, and transforming it as needed. This step involves handling missing values, removing duplicates, encoding categorical variables, and normalizing numerical features.

Step 4: Exploratory Data Analysis (EDA)

Perform EDA to understand the underlying patterns in the data. Visualizations, statistical summaries, and correlation analysis help identify relationships and inform feature selection. This step is crucial for gaining insights and guiding model development.

Step 5: Model Selection

Choose appropriate machine learning algorithms based on the problem type (classification, regression, clustering) and the characteristics of the dataset. Experiment with multiple algorithms to identify the best performing model.

Step 6: Model Training

Train the selected model using the training dataset. This involves feeding the model input features and their corresponding labels (in supervised learning) to learn the underlying patterns.

Step 7: Model Evaluation

Evaluate the trained model using the test dataset. Use appropriate evaluation metrics to assess model performance, ensuring that it generalizes well to unseen data.

Step 8: Hyperparameter Tuning

Optimize model performance by fine-tuning hyperparameters. Techniques like grid search or random search can help identify the best combination of parameters for your model.

Step 9: Deployment

Once satisfied with the model's performance, deploy it to a production environment where it can make predictions on new data. Ensure that monitoring and maintenance strategies are in place to address any issues that arise post-deployment.

Conclusion

Understanding the fundamentals of machine learning is crucial for anyone looking to explore this field. By grasping key concepts, types of learning, and the machine learning workflow, you will be better equipped to apply these principles in practical scenarios. As we continue to delve into the specifics of machine learning with Weka, the knowledge gained in this chapter will serve as a valuable foundation for implementing algorithms and developing predictive models effectively.

Chapter 6: Supervised Learning Algorithms

Overview of Supervised Learning

Supervised learning is a pivotal aspect of machine learning, where models are trained on labeled datasets. In this paradigm, the algorithm learns a mapping from input features to output labels, allowing it to make predictions on unseen data. This chapter explores several key supervised learning algorithms, discussing their mechanics, advantages, disadvantages, and applications.

Key Characteristics of Supervised Learning

- **Labeled Data**: Supervised learning relies on datasets where each input feature vector is associated with a corresponding output label.
- **Prediction Capability**: The primary goal is to predict labels for new instances based on learned patterns from the training data.
- **Performance Evaluation**: The effectiveness of a supervised learning model is evaluated using metrics such as accuracy, precision, recall, and F1-score.

Linear Regression

Introduction

Linear regression is a foundational algorithm used for predicting continuous values. It models the relationship between one or more input features and a continuous output variable by fitting a linear equation to observed data.

Mechanics

The equation for a simple linear regression model can be expressed as:

$$y = \beta_0 + \beta_1 x_1 + \beta_2 x_2 + \ldots + \beta_n x_n + \epsilon$$

where:

- y is the predicted output,
- β_0 is the intercept,

- β_i are the coefficients for each feature x_i,
- ϵ is the error term.

The model parameters (β) are estimated using methods such as Ordinary Least Squares (OLS), which minimizes the sum of squared differences between the predicted and actual values.

Advantages

- **Simplicity**: Easy to understand and interpret.
- **Efficiency**: Computationally efficient for large datasets.
- **Predictive Power**: Works well when the relationship between features and the target variable is linear.

Disadvantages

- **Linearity Assumption**: Assumes a linear relationship, which may not hold in real-world scenarios.
- **Sensitivity to Outliers**: Outliers can significantly affect model predictions.

Applications

Linear regression is widely used in various domains, including finance (predicting stock prices), healthcare (estimating patient costs), and real estate (predicting property values).

Logistic Regression

Introduction

Logistic regression is a classification algorithm used to predict binary outcomes. It estimates the probability that a given instance belongs to a particular class, making it suitable for problems where the target variable is categorical.

Mechanics

The logistic regression model applies the logistic function (sigmoid) to the linear combination of input features:

$$P(y=1|x) = \frac{1}{1 + e^{-(\beta_0 + \beta_1 x_1 + \ldots + \beta_n x_n)}}$$

where:

- $P(y=1|x)$ is the probability of the positive class given features xxx,
- e is the base of the natural logarithm.

The model predicts the class label based on a threshold (commonly 0.5). If the predicted probability exceeds the threshold, the instance is classified as positive; otherwise, it is classified as negative.

Advantages

- **Interpretability**: Provides insights into feature importance through coefficient values.
- **Probabilistic Output**: Outputs probabilities, allowing for more nuanced decision-making.
- **Versatility**: Can be extended to multiclass problems using techniques like one-vs-all.

Disadvantages

- **Linearity Assumption**: Similar to linear regression, it assumes a linear relationship between features and the log-odds of the outcome.
- **Sensitive to Imbalanced Data**: Performance may degrade if the classes are imbalanced.

Applications

Logistic regression is commonly used in medical diagnostics (predicting disease presence), marketing (customer churn prediction), and credit scoring (loan approval).

Decision Trees

Introduction

Decision trees are a versatile algorithm used for both classification and regression tasks. They model decisions using a tree-like structure, where each internal node represents a feature, each branch represents a decision rule, and each leaf node represents an outcome.

Mechanics

The decision tree algorithm works by recursively splitting the data based on feature values to maximize information gain or minimize impurity (commonly measured using Gini impurity or entropy). The process continues until a stopping criterion is met (e.g., maximum depth, minimum samples per leaf).

Advantages

- **Interpretability**: Easy to visualize and interpret, making it accessible for non-experts.
- **Non-Linear Relationships**: Capable of capturing complex relationships between features.
- **No Need for Feature Scaling**: Decision trees do not require normalization or standardization of features.

Disadvantages

- **Overfitting**: Decision trees can easily overfit the training data, especially if not properly pruned.
- **Instability**: Small changes in data can lead to significantly different trees.

Applications

Decision trees are used in various applications, including loan approval (risk assessment), medical diagnosis (predicting disease types), and customer segmentation.

Support Vector Machines (SVM)

Introduction

Support Vector Machines (SVM) are powerful algorithms used for classification and regression tasks. They work by finding the optimal hyperplane that separates different classes in the feature space.

Mechanics

SVM aims to maximize the margin between classes while minimizing classification errors. The decision boundary (hyperplane) is defined by the support vectors—the data points closest to the boundary. The optimization problem can be formulated as:

$$\text{minimize } \frac{1}{2} ||w||^2 \text{ subject to } y_i(w \cdot x_i + b) \geq 1$$

where:

- www is the weight vector,
- bbb is the bias term,
- yiy_iyi is the class label for instance iii,
- xix_ixi are the feature vectors.

Advantages

- **Effective in High Dimensions**: SVM is particularly effective when dealing with high-dimensional data.
- **Robust to Overfitting**: By focusing on support vectors, SVM can generalize well to unseen data.
- **Kernel Trick**: The use of kernel functions allows SVM to handle non-linear relationships by transforming the input space.

Disadvantages

- **Computationally Intensive**: Training SVM models can be time-consuming for large datasets.
- **Choice of Kernel**: The performance heavily relies on the choice of kernel and its parameters.

Applications

SVM is widely used in image classification, text categorization, and bioinformatics (gene classification).

Neural Networks

Introduction

Neural networks are a class of algorithms inspired by the structure and function of the human brain. They consist of interconnected nodes (neurons) organized into layers, allowing them to learn complex patterns from data.

Mechanics

A basic neural network architecture consists of an input layer, one or more hidden layers, and an output layer. Each connection between neurons has an associated weight that is adjusted during training. The output of each neuron is computed using an activation function (e.g., ReLU, sigmoid).

Training a neural network involves using a process called backpropagation, which updates the weights based on the error of the predictions compared to the actual labels. The network is trained using optimization algorithms like stochastic gradient descent (SGD).

Advantages

- **Flexibility**: Neural networks can model complex, non-linear relationships, making them suitable for a wide range of applications.
- **Scalability**: They perform well on large datasets and can be adapted to various problem types (classification, regression).

Disadvantages

- **Complexity**: Neural networks require significant computational resources and expertise to tune hyperparameters effectively.
- **Interpretability**: They are often considered "black boxes," making it challenging to interpret how predictions are made.

Applications

Neural networks are extensively used in deep learning applications, such as image recognition, natural language processing, and speech recognition.

Conclusion

Supervised learning algorithms are integral to machine learning, offering various techniques to solve classification and regression problems. By understanding the mechanics, advantages, and applications of these algorithms, practitioners can choose the most appropriate methods for their specific tasks. As we progress in our exploration of machine learning with Weka, the knowledge gained in this chapter will serve as a foundation for implementing these algorithms effectively in practical scenarios.

Chapter 7: Unsupervised Learning Algorithms

Overview of Unsupervised Learning

Unsupervised learning is a crucial category of machine learning that deals with datasets that do not contain labeled outputs. In this approach, algorithms identify patterns, groupings, or structures within the data without explicit guidance. This chapter delves into key unsupervised learning algorithms, exploring their functionalities, advantages, disadvantages, and practical applications.

Key Characteristics of Unsupervised Learning

- **No Labeled Data**: Unsupervised learning works with datasets lacking predefined labels, making it ideal for exploratory analysis.
- **Pattern Discovery**: The primary goal is to uncover hidden patterns or structures within the data.
- **Dimensionality Reduction**: Unsupervised algorithms often reduce the complexity of data, aiding in visualization and interpretation.

Clustering Algorithms

Clustering is a fundamental unsupervised learning task that involves grouping similar data points together. Several clustering algorithms have been developed, each with distinct characteristics.

K-Means Clustering

Introduction

K-Means is one of the most widely used clustering algorithms. It partitions a dataset into kkk distinct clusters based on feature similarity.

Mechanics

1. **Initialization**: Select kkk initial centroids randomly from the dataset.
2. **Assignment Step**: Assign each data point to the nearest centroid, forming clusters.

3. **Update Step**: Recalculate centroids by taking the mean of all points in each cluster.
4. **Iterate**: Repeat the assignment and update steps until convergence (i.e., no changes in cluster assignments).

Advantages

- **Simplicity**: Easy to implement and understand.
- **Efficiency**: Computationally efficient for large datasets, especially with the use of techniques like the Elbow Method for choosing kkk.

Disadvantages

- **Choice of kkk**: The need to specify the number of clusters kkk beforehand can be challenging.
- **Sensitivity to Outliers**: Outliers can skew centroids, leading to misleading clusters.

Applications

K-Means is used in market segmentation, document clustering, and image compression.

Hierarchical Clustering

Introduction

Hierarchical clustering creates a tree-like structure (dendrogram) that represents the arrangement of clusters. It can be agglomerative (bottom-up) or divisive (top-down).

Mechanics

1. **Agglomerative Approach**:
   - Start with each data point as a separate cluster.
   - Iteratively merge the closest clusters based on a distance metric (e.g., Euclidean distance).
   - Continue until all points are merged into a single cluster or a desired number of clusters is reached.
2. **Divisive Approach**:
   - Start with one cluster containing all data points.
   - Recursively split clusters based on distance until each point is in its own cluster.

Advantages

- **No Need for Predefined Clusters**: The number of clusters is not specified in advance, allowing for flexibility.
- **Dendrogram Visualization**: The dendrogram provides insights into the data's hierarchical structure.

Disadvantages

- **Computationally Intensive**: Hierarchical clustering can be slow for large datasets due to its complexity.
- **Sensitivity to Noise**: Outliers can disproportionately affect the structure of the resulting clusters.

Applications

Hierarchical clustering is often used in social network analysis, gene expression data analysis, and organizational structure mapping.

Dimensionality Reduction Algorithms

Dimensionality reduction aims to reduce the number of features in a dataset while preserving essential information. This process enhances computational efficiency and helps mitigate the curse of dimensionality.

Principal Component Analysis (PCA)

Introduction

PCA is a widely used technique for dimensionality reduction. It transforms the original features into a new set of orthogonal features (principal components) that capture the maximum variance in the data.

Mechanics

1. **Standardization**: Scale the dataset to have a mean of 0 and a standard deviation of 1.
2. **Covariance Matrix**: Compute the covariance matrix to understand how variables relate to one another.
3. **Eigenvalue Decomposition**: Calculate the eigenvalues and eigenvectors of the covariance matrix to identify principal components.
4. **Select Components**: Choose the top kkk principal components based on their eigenvalues, which represent the variance explained.

Advantages

- **Variance Preservation**: PCA retains the most significant features that contribute to variance, simplifying data analysis.
- **Noise Reduction**: By eliminating less important components, PCA can enhance model performance.

Disadvantages

- **Linear Assumption**: PCA assumes linear relationships among features, which may not always hold true.
- **Interpretability**: The resulting components may be challenging to interpret in terms of the original features.

Applications

PCA is frequently used in image compression, exploratory data analysis, and feature reduction before applying supervised learning algorithms.

t-Distributed Stochastic Neighbor Embedding (t-SNE)

Introduction

t-SNE is a powerful technique for visualizing high-dimensional data in lower dimensions, particularly effective for preserving local structure.

Mechanics

1. **Pairwise Similarities**: Calculate pairwise similarities between data points in the high-dimensional space using a Gaussian distribution.
2. **Low-Dimensional Mapping**: Use a Student's t-distribution to compute pairwise similarities in the low-dimensional space, focusing on preserving the relationships between close points.
3. **Optimization**: Minimize the Kullback-Leibler divergence between the two distributions using gradient descent.

Advantages

- **Effective Visualization**: t-SNE excels at revealing clusters and patterns in high-dimensional data, making it ideal for exploratory analysis.
- **Preservation of Local Structure**: It effectively preserves local relationships, making clusters more distinct in the visualization.

Disadvantages

- **Computational Complexity**: t-SNE can be computationally intensive, especially for large datasets.
- **Parameter Sensitivity**: The choice of perplexity and other hyperparameters can significantly affect the results.

Applications

t-SNE is widely used in fields like genomics, image analysis, and natural language processing for visualizing complex datasets.

Association Rule Learning

Association rule learning identifies interesting relationships between variables in large datasets. It is particularly useful for market basket analysis, where the goal is to discover product associations.

Apriori Algorithm

Introduction

The Apriori algorithm is a classic algorithm for mining frequent itemsets and generating association rules.

Mechanics

1. **Frequent Itemsets**: Identify itemsets that appear frequently in transactions using a user-defined minimum support threshold.
2. **Rule Generation**: Generate rules from the frequent itemsets based on a minimum confidence threshold, which indicates how often the rule holds true.

Advantages

- **Simplicity**: The algorithm is straightforward and easy to implement.
- **Interpretability**: The generated rules are easy to understand and communicate.

Disadvantages

- **Scalability**: The algorithm may struggle with very large datasets due to its computational requirements.
- **Low Efficiency**: The need to scan the dataset multiple times can lead to inefficiencies.

Applications

The Apriori algorithm is commonly used in market basket analysis, recommendation systems, and customer segmentation.

FP-Growth Algorithm

Introduction

The FP-Growth algorithm is an alternative to Apriori that addresses its limitations by using a more efficient data structure called the FP-tree.

Mechanics

1. **FP-Tree Construction**: Build a compact tree structure that encodes the frequency of itemsets without generating candidate sets.
2. **Frequent Pattern Mining**: Recursively mine the FP-tree to extract frequent itemsets, avoiding multiple dataset scans.

Advantages

- **Efficiency**: FP-Growth is generally faster than Apriori, especially on large datasets, due to reduced computation.
- **Single Dataset Scan**: It scans the dataset only once to construct the FP-tree.

Disadvantages

- **Complexity**: The FP-tree structure can be complex to implement and understand.
- **Memory Consumption**: For very large datasets, FP-trees can consume significant memory.

Applications

FP-Growth is used in various applications, including market basket analysis, web usage mining, and social network analysis.

Conclusion

Unsupervised learning algorithms play a vital role in machine learning, enabling the discovery of patterns and structures in unlabeled data. By understanding key algorithms such as K-Means, hierarchical clustering, PCA, and association rule learning, practitioners can effectively explore and analyze data, uncovering valuable insights. This foundational knowledge will serve as a crucial element as we continue to implement and utilize these techniques with Weka in practical scenarios.

Chapter 8: Model Evaluation and Validation Techniques

Overview of Model Evaluation

Model evaluation is a critical aspect of the machine learning workflow, ensuring that models perform well on unseen data. Effective evaluation helps determine the quality and reliability of predictions made by machine learning algorithms. This chapter explores various techniques for evaluating and validating models, emphasizing the importance of metrics, methodologies, and best practices.

Importance of Model Evaluation

Evaluating machine learning models is essential for several reasons:

- **Performance Assessment**: It provides insights into how well the model performs on unseen data.
- **Model Selection**: It helps in choosing the best model among multiple candidates based on defined criteria.
- **Avoiding Overfitting**: Proper evaluation techniques can mitigate the risk of overfitting, ensuring the model generalizes well.

Evaluation Metrics

Evaluation metrics differ based on the type of problem (classification or regression). Understanding these metrics is crucial for interpreting model performance.

Classification Metrics

1. **Accuracy**: The ratio of correctly predicted instances to the total instances. It provides a general measure of performance.
$$\text{Accuracy} = \frac{\text{True Positives} + \text{True Negatives}}{\text{Total Instances}}$$
2. **Precision**: The ratio of correctly predicted positive instances to the total predicted positives. It indicates the accuracy of positive predictions.
$$\text{Precision} = \frac{\text{True Positives}}{\text{True Positives} + \text{False Positives}}$$

3. **Recall (Sensitivity)**: The ratio of correctly predicted positive instances to the actual positives. It measures the model's ability to find all relevant cases.
$$\text{Recall} = \frac{\text{True Positives}}{\text{True Positives} + \text{False Negatives}}$$
4. **F1-Score**: The harmonic mean of precision and recall, providing a balance between the two metrics.
$$F1 = 2 \times \frac{\text{Precision} \times \text{Recall}}{\text{Precision} + \text{Recall}}$$
5. **Receiver Operating Characteristic (ROC) Curve and Area Under the Curve (AUC)**: The ROC curve plots the true positive rate against the false positive rate. AUC quantifies the overall ability of the model to distinguish between classes.

Regression Metrics

1. **Mean Absolute Error (MAE)**: The average of the absolute errors between predicted and actual values. It provides a straightforward interpretation of prediction accuracy.
$$\text{MAE} = \frac{1}{n} \sum_{i=1}^{n} |y_i - \hat{y}_i|$$
2. **Mean Squared Error (MSE)**: The average of the squared errors between predicted and actual values. It penalizes larger errors more significantly.
$$\text{MSE} = \frac{1}{n} \sum_{i=1}^{n} (y_i - \hat{y}_i)^2$$
3. **Root Mean Squared Error (RMSE)**: The square root of the MSE, providing a measure of error in the same units as the target variable.
$$\text{RMSE} = \sqrt{\text{MSE}}$$
4. **R-squared**: The proportion of variance in the dependent variable that can be explained by the independent variables. It ranges from 0 to 1, with higher values indicating a better fit.
$$R^2 = 1 - \frac{\sum_{i=1}^{n} (y_i - \hat{y}_i)^2}{\sum_{i=1}^{n} (y_i - \bar{y})^2}$$

Cross-Validation Techniques

Cross-validation is a vital technique for assessing model performance and generalization ability. It involves partitioning the dataset into subsets for training and testing multiple times.

K-Fold Cross-Validation

K-Fold Cross-Validation divides the dataset into k equal subsets (folds). The model is trained on $k-1$ folds and validated on the remaining fold. This process is repeated k times, with each fold serving as the test set once. The final performance metric is averaged across all folds, providing a robust estimate of the model's performance.

Advantages

- **Bias Reduction**: By using multiple train-test splits, K-Fold reduces the bias associated with a single train-test split.
- **Utilization of Data**: It maximizes the use of available data, especially beneficial for smaller datasets.

Disadvantages

- **Computationally Intensive**: Training the model k times can be time-consuming, particularly with complex models.

Stratified K-Fold Cross-Validation

Stratified K-Fold ensures that each fold has the same proportion of class labels as the original dataset, making it particularly useful for imbalanced classification tasks. It mitigates the risk of skewed performance estimates that can occur in regular K-Fold.

Leave-One-Out Cross-Validation (LOOCV)

LOOCV is a special case of K-Fold where k is equal to the number of instances in the dataset. Each iteration trains the model on all but one instance, using the remaining instance for validation. This method provides a very thorough evaluation but can be extremely computationally intensive for large datasets.

Train-Test Split

The simplest evaluation method involves dividing the dataset into two subsets: a training set and a test set. The model is trained on the training set and evaluated on the test set. While straightforward, this method can lead to high variance in performance estimates, as results depend heavily on how the data is split.

Bias-Variance Tradeoff

Understanding the bias-variance tradeoff is essential for evaluating model performance.

- **Bias** refers to the error due to overly simplistic assumptions in the learning algorithm, leading to underfitting.
- **Variance** refers to the error due to excessive complexity in the model, causing it to learn noise from the training data and resulting in overfitting.

A good model strikes a balance between bias and variance, minimizing total error on unseen data.

Best Practices for Model Evaluation

1. **Use Multiple Metrics**: Different metrics provide various perspectives on model performance. For classification, consider accuracy, precision, recall, and F1-score together. For regression, use MAE, MSE, and R-squared.
2. **Perform Cross-Validation**: Use cross-validation techniques to obtain a robust estimate of model performance and generalization.
3. **Visualize Results**: Visualizations, such as ROC curves and confusion matrices, can provide deeper insights into model performance and potential issues.
4. **Be Aware of Data Leakage**: Ensure that information from the test set does not influence the training process, as this can lead to overly optimistic performance estimates.
5. **Document Evaluation Procedures**: Maintain clear documentation of evaluation methodologies and results to ensure reproducibility and transparency.

Conclusion

Model evaluation and validation techniques are essential for developing reliable machine learning models. By understanding various evaluation metrics, cross-validation methods, and the bias-variance tradeoff, practitioners can ensure that their models perform well on unseen data. This foundational knowledge will guide effective evaluation strategies as we delve deeper into implementing and optimizing machine learning models with Weka in practical applications.

Chapter 9: Feature Selection and Dimensionality Reduction

Overview of Feature Selection and Dimensionality Reduction

Feature selection and dimensionality reduction are critical processes in the machine learning pipeline. They enhance model performance by reducing the complexity of datasets and mitigating issues such as overfitting and high computational costs. This chapter explores the concepts, techniques, and best practices associated with feature selection and dimensionality reduction, highlighting their importance in building robust machine learning models.

Importance of Feature Selection and Dimensionality Reduction

1. **Improved Model Performance**: By eliminating irrelevant or redundant features, models can focus on the most informative aspects of the data, leading to better performance and generalization.
2. **Reduced Overfitting**: Fewer features can reduce the risk of overfitting, as models are less likely to learn noise in the data.
3. **Decreased Computational Cost**: Reducing the number of features decreases the time and resources required for training, making models more efficient.
4. **Enhanced Interpretability**: Simplifying the model with fewer features can make it easier to understand and communicate insights derived from the data.

Feature Selection Techniques

Feature selection involves selecting a subset of relevant features for model building. Various techniques can be employed, classified into three main categories: filter methods, wrapper methods, and embedded methods.

Filter Methods

Filter methods assess the relevance of features independently of the model. They use statistical measures to evaluate the importance of each feature.

1. **Correlation Coefficient**: Measures the linear relationship between each feature and the target variable. Features with low correlation may be considered irrelevant.
2. **Chi-Squared Test**: Evaluates the independence of categorical features concerning the target variable. A high chi-squared statistic indicates a significant relationship.
3. **Mutual Information**: Measures the amount of information gained about the target variable through the feature. Higher mutual information suggests a stronger relationship.

Advantages of Filter Methods

- **Speed**: They are computationally efficient, making them suitable for large datasets.
- **Model Agnostic**: They can be applied regardless of the machine learning model being used.

Disadvantages of Filter Methods

- **Independence Assumption**: They evaluate features in isolation, potentially overlooking interactions between features.

Wrapper Methods

Wrapper methods evaluate feature subsets by training and testing a model on them. They use the model's performance as a criterion for selecting features.

1. **Forward Selection**: Starts with an empty set of features and adds features iteratively based on performance improvement.
2. **Backward Elimination**: Starts with all features and removes the least significant features iteratively.
3. **Recursive Feature Elimination (RFE)**: Trains the model multiple times, removing the least important features in each iteration until the desired number of features is reached.

Advantages of Wrapper Methods

- **Interaction Consideration**: They account for feature interactions, providing potentially better feature subsets.

Disadvantages of Wrapper Methods

- **Computationally Intensive**: They require multiple model evaluations, making them less efficient, especially for large datasets.

Embedded Methods

Embedded methods incorporate feature selection within the model training process. They perform feature selection as part of the model fitting procedure.

1. **Lasso Regression**: Applies L1 regularization to reduce the coefficients of less important features to zero, effectively selecting a subset of features.
2. **Tree-Based Methods**: Algorithms like Random Forests and Gradient Boosting inherently perform feature selection by evaluating feature importance during training.

Advantages of Embedded Methods

- **Efficiency**: They combine feature selection and model training, making them more efficient than wrapper methods.
- **Model Specific**: They can provide tailored feature selection based on the characteristics of the model.

Disadvantages of Embedded Methods

- **Model Dependency**: Feature selection is tied to a specific model, which may not generalize well to other algorithms.

Dimensionality Reduction Techniques

Dimensionality reduction involves transforming data into a lower-dimensional space while retaining essential information. This can be achieved through various techniques.

Principal Component Analysis (PCA)

PCA is one of the most widely used dimensionality reduction techniques. It transforms the original features into a set of orthogonal components that capture the maximum variance.

1. **Standardization**: Scale the data to have a mean of 0 and a standard deviation of 1.
2. **Covariance Matrix Calculation**: Compute the covariance matrix to understand relationships among features.

3. **Eigenvalue Decomposition**: Identify the eigenvectors and eigenvalues of the covariance matrix, which determine the principal components.
4. **Component Selection**: Select the top kkk principal components that explain the most variance.

Advantages of PCA

- **Variance Preservation**: It retains the most important aspects of the data, aiding in visualization and interpretation.
- **Noise Reduction**: By eliminating less important components, PCA can improve model performance.

Disadvantages of PCA

- **Linear Assumption**: PCA assumes linear relationships among features, which may not always be valid.
- **Interpretability**: The transformed components can be challenging to relate back to original features.

t-Distributed Stochastic Neighbor Embedding (t-SNE)

t-SNE is particularly useful for visualizing high-dimensional data in lower dimensions while preserving local structures.

1. **Pairwise Similarities**: Calculate similarities between data points in the high-dimensional space using a Gaussian distribution.
2. **Low-Dimensional Mapping**: Map these points to a lower-dimensional space using a Student's t-distribution to focus on preserving local relationships.
3. **Optimization**: Use gradient descent to minimize the Kullback-Leibler divergence between the two distributions.

Advantages of t-SNE

- **Effective Visualization**: It excels at revealing clusters in high-dimensional datasets.
- **Local Structure Preservation**: It maintains local relationships, enhancing interpretability.

Disadvantages of t-SNE

- **Computationally Intensive**: It can be slow, especially for large datasets.
- **Parameter Sensitivity**: The results can vary significantly based on hyperparameter choices.

Linear Discriminant Analysis (LDA)

LDA is a technique for both classification and dimensionality reduction. It focuses on maximizing class separability.

1. **Compute Class Means**: Calculate the mean of each class and the overall mean.
2. **Within-Class and Between-Class Matrices**: Calculate these matrices to assess the variance within and between classes.
3. **Eigenvalue Decomposition**: Perform eigenvalue decomposition to identify the directions that maximize class separation.
4. **Transform Data**: Project the data onto the identified directions, reducing dimensionality.

Advantages of LDA

- **Class Separation**: It explicitly focuses on maximizing class separation, which can enhance classification performance.
- **Interpretability**: The resulting components can be easier to interpret in relation to class labels.

Disadvantages of LDA

- **Assumptions**: It assumes normally distributed classes and equal covariance matrices, which may not hold in practice.

Best Practices for Feature Selection and Dimensionality Reduction

1. **Understand the Data**: Explore and analyze the dataset before applying selection or reduction techniques to identify relevant features.
2. **Combine Techniques**: Consider using a combination of feature selection and dimensionality reduction methods for optimal results.
3. **Evaluate Performance**: Assess the impact of feature selection and dimensionality reduction on model performance using appropriate metrics.
4. **Iterative Process**: Feature selection and dimensionality reduction should be iterative processes, refining the approach based on model feedback.
5. **Domain Knowledge**: Leverage domain expertise to inform feature selection and understand the relevance of features.

Conclusion

Feature selection and dimensionality reduction are essential processes in machine learning that enhance model performance and efficiency. By understanding various techniques, their advantages and disadvantages, and best practices, practitioners can effectively streamline their models and improve predictive capabilities. This foundational knowledge will support the implementation of these strategies using Weka, enabling practitioners to build more robust and interpretable machine learning models.

Chapter 10: Ensemble Learning Methods

Overview of Ensemble Learning

Ensemble learning is a powerful technique in machine learning that combines multiple models to produce improved predictions. By aggregating the strengths of various algorithms, ensemble methods can significantly enhance accuracy, robustness, and generalization. This chapter explores the different ensemble learning methods, their advantages, disadvantages, and practical applications.

Importance of Ensemble Learning

1. **Increased Accuracy**: Ensemble methods can outperform individual models by leveraging diverse learning algorithms or subsets of data.
2. **Robustness**: By combining multiple models, ensembles can reduce the risk of overfitting and improve performance on unseen data.
3. **Handling Variability**: Ensemble methods can mitigate the effects of noise and outliers by averaging predictions from multiple models.

Types of Ensemble Learning Methods

Ensemble learning methods are broadly categorized into two main types: bagging and boosting.

Bagging (Bootstrap Aggregating)

Bagging is an ensemble technique that aims to reduce variance by training multiple models independently on random subsets of the training data. The predictions of these models are then aggregated, typically through averaging (for regression) or voting (for classification).

Key Characteristics

1. **Random Sampling**: Bagging involves creating multiple bootstrap samples (random samples with replacement) from the training dataset.
2. **Independence**: Each model is trained independently, allowing for diverse predictions.
3. **Aggregation**: The final prediction is made by aggregating the predictions from all models.

Common Algorithms

1. **Random Forests**: An extension of bagging that constructs a multitude of decision trees. Each tree is trained on a random subset of the data, and the final prediction is made by majority voting or averaging the predictions from all trees.
2. **Bagged Decision Trees**: Involves training individual decision trees on different bootstrap samples and aggregating their predictions.

Advantages of Bagging

- **Variance Reduction**: By averaging predictions, bagging reduces the model's variance and helps avoid overfitting.
- **Robustness**: Bagging is particularly effective in stabilizing models that are prone to high variance, such as decision trees.

Disadvantages of Bagging

- **Bias Retention**: While bagging reduces variance, it may not significantly reduce bias, especially if the base models are weak learners.

Boosting

Boosting is another ensemble technique that focuses on improving the performance of weak learners by combining them sequentially. Unlike bagging, boosting trains models iteratively, with each new model attempting to correct the errors made by the previous models.

Key Characteristics

1. **Sequential Training**: Each model is trained on the errors made by the previous models, emphasizing misclassified instances.
2. **Weighting**: Instances that are misclassified are given more weight in subsequent models, allowing the ensemble to focus on hard-to-predict samples.
3. **Aggregation**: The final prediction is typically a weighted sum of the predictions from all models.

Common Algorithms

1. **AdaBoost (Adaptive Boosting)**: It assigns weights to instances and updates these weights after each iteration. Weak classifiers are combined to create a strong classifier, with more emphasis placed on misclassified instances.
2. **Gradient Boosting**: It builds models sequentially, each one correcting the errors of the previous one. It optimizes a loss function through gradient descent.

3. **XGBoost**: An optimized implementation of gradient boosting that is faster and more efficient, with built-in regularization to prevent overfitting.

Advantages of Boosting

- **High Accuracy**: Boosting can yield very accurate predictions, often outperforming other methods.
- **Focus on Difficult Cases**: By emphasizing misclassified instances, boosting can effectively handle challenging datasets.

Disadvantages of Boosting

- **Sensitivity to Noise**: Boosting can be sensitive to noisy data and outliers, as it focuses on correcting misclassifications.
- **Overfitting Risk**: Without proper tuning, boosting algorithms can overfit the training data.

Ensemble Learning Strategies

Voting

Voting is a straightforward ensemble strategy where multiple models vote on the final prediction. It can be classified into two types:

1. **Hard Voting**: Each model casts a vote for a class label, and the class with the majority votes is selected.
2. **Soft Voting**: Probabilities from each model are averaged, and the class with the highest average probability is selected. This method often leads to better performance, especially when models provide calibrated probabilities.

Stacking

Stacking is an ensemble method that involves training multiple base models and combining their predictions using a meta-model. The base models can be of different types, and their predictions serve as input features for the meta-model.

Key Characteristics

1. **Diverse Models**: Stacking allows the use of various algorithms, capitalizing on their individual strengths.
2. **Meta-Learning**: A new model is trained to learn how to best combine the predictions from base models.

Advantages of Stacking

- **Flexibility**: It can combine various types of models, leading to improved performance.
- **Learning from Errors**: The meta-model can learn how to correct the mistakes of base models, enhancing overall predictions.

Disadvantages of Stacking

- **Complexity**: Stacking can be more complex to implement and requires careful tuning.
- **Risk of Overfitting**: If the meta-model is overly complex, it may overfit the training data.

Practical Applications of Ensemble Learning

Ensemble learning methods are widely used across various domains due to their effectiveness:

1. **Finance**: In credit scoring and risk assessment, ensemble methods improve predictions of loan defaults and creditworthiness.
2. **Healthcare**: Ensemble models can enhance disease diagnosis and prognosis predictions by integrating diverse data sources.
3. **Image and Speech Recognition**: Combining multiple models can significantly boost accuracy in recognizing objects in images or transcribing spoken words.
4. **Marketing**: Ensemble learning helps in customer segmentation and targeting by improving the accuracy of predictive models.

Best Practices for Ensemble Learning

1. **Diversity is Key**: Use a diverse set of base models to leverage different strengths and minimize error correlation.
2. **Tune Hyperparameters**: Proper tuning of hyperparameters is crucial for maximizing the performance of ensemble methods.
3. **Cross-Validation**: Employ cross-validation to evaluate the performance of the ensemble and ensure its robustness.
4. **Feature Engineering**: Invest time in feature engineering, as the quality of features can significantly impact ensemble performance.
5. **Monitor Performance**: Continuously monitor the ensemble model's performance and adjust as necessary to maintain accuracy over time.

Conclusion

Ensemble learning methods offer powerful techniques for improving the performance of machine learning models. By understanding different approaches like bagging and boosting, practitioners can leverage the strengths of multiple models to achieve better accuracy and robustness. This foundational knowledge will support the implementation of ensemble techniques in practical applications using Weka, enabling the development of highly effective machine learning solutions.

Chapter 11: Neural Networks and Deep Learning with Java

Overview of Neural Networks and Deep Learning

Neural networks and deep learning represent a powerful class of machine learning algorithms inspired by the structure and function of the human brain. They have gained immense popularity due to their ability to model complex patterns in data and have revolutionized various fields, including computer vision, natural language processing, and more. This chapter explores the fundamentals of neural networks, the principles of deep learning, and how these concepts can be implemented in Java.

Importance of Neural Networks and Deep Learning

1. **Complex Pattern Recognition**: Neural networks excel at identifying intricate relationships within data, making them suitable for tasks like image and speech recognition.
2. **Scalability**: Deep learning models can handle large datasets effectively, leveraging the computational power of modern hardware.
3. **Feature Learning**: Unlike traditional algorithms that rely on handcrafted features, deep learning automatically extracts relevant features from raw data.
4. **Versatility**: Neural networks can be applied across diverse domains, including finance, healthcare, and entertainment, enabling a wide range of applications.

Fundamentals of Neural Networks

Structure of a Neural Network

A neural network consists of interconnected nodes (neurons) organized into layers:

1. **Input Layer**: The first layer that receives the input features. Each node corresponds to a feature in the dataset.
2. **Hidden Layers**: Intermediate layers that process inputs and capture patterns. A network can have one or more hidden layers.
3. **Output Layer**: The final layer that produces the output. For classification tasks, each node corresponds to a class label.

Activation Functions

Activation functions introduce non-linearity into the model, enabling it to learn complex patterns. Common activation functions include:

1. **Sigmoid**: Maps input values to a range between 0 and 1. Suitable for binary classification but can cause vanishing gradient issues.
2. **Tanh**: Similar to sigmoid but maps values to a range between -1 and 1. Generally performs better than sigmoid.
3. **ReLU (Rectified Linear Unit)**: Outputs the input directly if positive; otherwise, it outputs zero. Widely used in hidden layers due to its efficiency and ability to mitigate vanishing gradient problems.
4. **Softmax**: Used in the output layer for multi-class classification, converting logits into probabilities for each class.

Forward Propagation

Forward propagation is the process of passing input data through the network to generate an output. It involves:

1. **Weighted Sum**: Each neuron computes a weighted sum of its inputs.
2. **Activation Function**: The weighted sum is then passed through an activation function to produce the neuron's output.
3. **Layer-by-Layer Propagation**: This process is repeated layer by layer until the final output is obtained.

Loss Function

The loss function measures the discrepancy between the predicted output and the actual target. Common loss functions include:

1. **Mean Squared Error (MSE)**: Used for regression tasks, calculating the average squared difference between predicted and actual values.
2. **Cross-Entropy Loss**: Used for classification tasks, measuring the performance of a model whose output is a probability value between 0 and 1.

Backpropagation

Backpropagation is the algorithm used to update the weights of the network during training. It involves:

1. **Calculating the Loss Gradient**: Compute the gradient of the loss function concerning each weight in the network.

2. **Updating Weights**: Adjust the weights using optimization algorithms (e.g., stochastic gradient descent) based on the computed gradients.

Deep Learning Concepts

Deep Neural Networks (DNN)

Deep neural networks are networks with multiple hidden layers, enabling them to learn hierarchical representations of data. Each layer captures increasingly abstract features, leading to better performance on complex tasks.

Convolutional Neural Networks (CNN)

CNNs are specialized for processing grid-like data, such as images. Key features include:

1. **Convolutional Layers**: Apply filters (kernels) to the input to extract spatial features.
2. **Pooling Layers**: Downsample the output, reducing dimensionality while retaining important features.
3. **Fully Connected Layers**: Connect every neuron in one layer to every neuron in the next layer, typically used in the final stages for classification.

Recurrent Neural Networks (RNN)

RNNs are designed for sequential data, such as time series or natural language. They maintain a hidden state that captures information from previous time steps, allowing them to model dependencies in sequences.

1. **LSTM (Long Short-Term Memory)**: A type of RNN that mitigates the vanishing gradient problem by using memory cells and gating mechanisms to control information flow.
2. **GRU (Gated Recurrent Unit)**: A simplified version of LSTM that uses fewer gates while maintaining performance.

Transfer Learning

Transfer learning leverages pre-trained models on large datasets to boost performance on related tasks. This approach is particularly useful when labeled data is scarce for the target task.

Implementing Neural Networks in Java

Libraries for Neural Networks in Java

Java offers several libraries for implementing neural networks and deep learning:

1. **Deeplearning4j**: A popular open-source deep learning library that provides a robust framework for building neural networks in Java. It supports a wide range of architectures, including CNNs and RNNs.
2. **DL4J**: Integrated with Apache Spark, enabling distributed training and large-scale data processing.
3. **Neuroph**: A lightweight Java framework for developing neural networks, suitable for beginners and smaller projects.
4. **Java-ML**: A library focused on machine learning algorithms, including basic neural network implementations.

Building a Neural Network with Deeplearning4j

To illustrate the process of building a neural network, let's consider a simple example using Deeplearning4j.

1. **Setting Up the Environment**: Install Java and the Deeplearning4j library. Ensure all dependencies are correctly configured.
2. **Preparing the Dataset**: Load and preprocess your dataset. This typically involves normalizing input features and splitting the data into training and testing sets.

Creating the Network Configuration: Define the architecture of the neural network. Here's an example configuration for a feedforward neural network:

java
Copy code
```
MultiLayerConfiguration config = new NeuralNetConfiguration.Builder()
    .seed(123) // For reproducibility
    .updater(new Adam(0.001)) // Optimizer
    .list()
        .layer(new DenseLayer.Builder().nIn(inputSize).nOut(hiddenSize).activation(Activation.RELU).build())
```

```
                                            .layer(new
OutputLayer.Builder(LossFunctions.LossFunction.NEGATIVELOGLIKELI
HOOD)
            .activation(Activation.SOFTMAX)
            .nIn(hiddenSize)
            .nOut(outputSize)
            .build())
        .build();
```

3.

Training the Model: Create a MultiLayerNetwork object and train it using the training dataset.
java
Copy code
```
MultiLayerNetwork model = new MultiLayerNetwork(config);
model.init();
model.fit(trainingData);
```

4.

Evaluating the Model: After training, evaluate the model's performance on the test set using appropriate metrics.
java
Copy code
```
Evaluation evaluation = model.evaluate(testData);
System.out.println(evaluation.stats());
```

5.

Challenges in Neural Network Training

1. **Overfitting**: When a model performs well on training data but poorly on unseen data. Techniques such as dropout, early stopping, and regularization can help mitigate overfitting.
2. **Vanishing/Exploding Gradients**: Deep networks may suffer from gradients becoming too small (vanishing) or too large (exploding) during backpropagation. Using activation functions like ReLU and proper weight initialization can alleviate these issues.

3. **Hyperparameter Tuning**: Choosing the right architecture, learning rate, batch size, and other hyperparameters is crucial for optimal performance. Techniques such as grid search or random search can be used to find the best settings.
4. **Computational Resources**: Training deep neural networks can be resource-intensive. Utilizing GPUs and distributed computing can significantly speed up the training process.

Best Practices for Neural Network Development

1. **Start Simple**: Begin with a simple model before experimenting with complex architectures.
2. **Preprocessing**: Carefully preprocess data to enhance model performance. Normalization, handling missing values, and feature engineering are vital steps.
3. **Monitor Training**: Keep track of training and validation metrics to detect overfitting early.
4. **Experimentation**: Be prepared to experiment with different architectures, activation functions, and optimization algorithms to find the best solution.
5. **Documentation**: Maintain clear documentation of model configurations, training procedures, and evaluation results for reproducibility and future reference.

Conclusion

Neural networks and deep learning have transformed the landscape of machine learning by providing powerful tools for modeling complex data patterns. With a solid understanding of the underlying principles and practical implementation strategies in Java, practitioners can harness the capabilities of deep learning for a wide range of applications. This foundational knowledge will support further exploration and application of neural networks using Weka, empowering the development of advanced machine learning solutions.

Chapter 12: Model Evaluation and Hyperparameter Tuning

Overview of Model Evaluation and Hyperparameter Tuning

Model evaluation and hyperparameter tuning are essential components of the machine learning process, ensuring that models are robust, accurate, and generalizable to new data. Effective evaluation techniques help quantify model performance, while careful tuning of hyperparameters enhances predictive capability. This chapter explores various evaluation metrics, validation strategies, and hyperparameter tuning methods, focusing on practical applications using Java libraries such as Weka.

Importance of Model Evaluation

1. **Performance Assessment**: Evaluating a model helps determine how well it performs on unseen data, providing insights into its predictive capabilities.
2. **Model Selection**: By comparing the performance of multiple models, practitioners can select the most appropriate one for a given task.
3. **Overfitting Detection**: Evaluation helps identify overfitting, where a model performs well on training data but poorly on validation or test data.
4. **Benchmarking**: Establishing baseline performance metrics enables further improvements and progress tracking.

Model Evaluation Metrics

Selecting appropriate evaluation metrics is crucial for assessing model performance. The choice of metric depends on the specific problem (classification or regression) and the goals of the analysis.

Classification Metrics

1. **Accuracy**: The proportion of correct predictions among the total number of predictions. It is useful for balanced datasets but can be misleading in cases of class imbalance.
$$\text{Accuracy} = \frac{\text{TP} + \text{TN}}{\text{TP} + \text{TN} + \text{FP} + \text{FN}}$$

2. **Precision**: The proportion of true positive predictions among all positive predictions. High precision indicates that most predicted positive instances are indeed positive.
$$\text{Precision} = \frac{\text{TP}}{\text{TP} + \text{FP}}$$
3. **Recall (Sensitivity)**: The proportion of true positive predictions among all actual positive instances. High recall indicates that most actual positives are correctly identified.
$$\text{Recall} = \frac{\text{TP}}{\text{TP} + \text{FN}}$$
4. **F1 Score**: The harmonic mean of precision and recall, providing a balance between the two metrics. It is particularly useful in situations where one metric may be prioritized over the other.
$$\text{F1 Score} = 2 \times \frac{\text{Precision} \times \text{Recall}}{\text{Precision} + \text{Recall}}$$
5. **ROC Curve and AUC**: The Receiver Operating Characteristic (ROC) curve plots the true positive rate against the false positive rate at various threshold settings. The Area Under the Curve (AUC) quantifies the overall performance of the model, with values closer to 1 indicating better performance.

Regression Metrics

1. **Mean Absolute Error (MAE)**: The average of the absolute differences between predicted and actual values. MAE provides a straightforward interpretation of prediction accuracy.
$$\text{MAE} = \frac{1}{n} \sum_{i=1}^{n} |y_i - \hat{y}_i|$$
2. **Mean Squared Error (MSE)**: The average of the squared differences between predicted and actual values. MSE penalizes larger errors more than MAE, making it sensitive to outliers.
$$\text{MSE} = \frac{1}{n} \sum_{i=1}^{n} (y_i - \hat{y}_i)^2$$
3. **Root Mean Squared Error (RMSE)**: The square root of MSE, providing an interpretable metric in the same units as the target variable.
$$\text{RMSE} = \sqrt{\text{MSE}}$$
4. **R-squared**: A statistical measure representing the proportion of variance for a dependent variable that can be explained by the independent variables. Values range from 0 to 1, with higher values indicating a better fit.

Model Validation Strategies

Validation strategies assess how well a model generalizes to unseen data. Common techniques include:

Train-Test Split

This method involves splitting the dataset into two subsets: one for training and one for testing. A typical split ratio is 80/20 or 70/30. This approach is simple but may lead to variance in results based on the random split.

Cross-Validation

Cross-validation is a more robust technique that reduces variance and provides a better assessment of model performance.

1. **K-Fold Cross-Validation**: The dataset is divided into kkk equally sized folds. The model is trained on k−1k-1k−1 folds and validated on the remaining fold. This process is repeated kkk times, with each fold serving as the validation set once. The results are averaged to obtain a comprehensive performance metric.
2. **Stratified K-Fold**: Similar to K-fold but ensures that each fold maintains the same class distribution as the original dataset, making it particularly useful for imbalanced datasets.

Leave-One-Out Cross-Validation (LOOCV)

In LOOCV, each sample in the dataset serves as a test set once while the remaining samples form the training set. While this method provides a comprehensive evaluation, it can be computationally expensive for large datasets.

Bootstrapping

Bootstrapping involves sampling with replacement to create multiple training datasets. Each model is trained on these datasets, and the predictions are averaged to generate a final prediction. This method can help assess model stability and variance.

Hyperparameter Tuning

Hyperparameters are parameters that are set before training and govern the learning process. Effective tuning of hyperparameters is crucial for optimizing model performance. Common strategies include:

Manual Search

This involves manually adjusting hyperparameters based on experience and intuition. While straightforward, it can be time-consuming and may not yield optimal results.

Grid Search

Grid search systematically evaluates a predefined set of hyperparameter combinations. It exhaustively searches through specified values for each hyperparameter, making it suitable for smaller search spaces.

1. **Implementation**: Use a library like Weka to configure grid search for specific hyperparameters. For example, tuning the learning rate and maximum depth of a decision tree.
2. **Pros and Cons**: Grid search ensures thorough exploration but can be computationally expensive for large search spaces.

Random Search

Random search samples hyperparameter values from specified distributions. It is often more efficient than grid search, especially for high-dimensional spaces.

1. **Advantages**: It can explore a broader range of values and is less prone to overfitting specific combinations.
2. **Disadvantages**: There is no guarantee that the best combination will be found, as it relies on randomness.

Bayesian Optimization

Bayesian optimization uses probabilistic models to identify the optimal hyperparameters by evaluating the performance of previous configurations. This approach is more efficient than grid and random searches.

1. **Sequential Decision Making**: It focuses on selecting the next hyperparameter configuration based on past evaluations, allowing for more informed decisions.
2. **Complexity**: While effective, it requires a deeper understanding of probabilistic modeling.

Use of Libraries for Tuning

Many Java libraries facilitate hyperparameter tuning. For example, Weka includes capabilities for performing grid search, random search, and even integration with other tuning libraries.

java
Copy code
```
// Example of using Weka for Grid Search
GridSearch grid = new GridSearch();
grid.setClassifier(new J48()); // Decision Tree Classifier
grid.addEvaluationMetric("accuracy");
grid.addParameter("C", Arrays.asList("0.1", "1.0", "10.0"));
grid.addParameter("M", Arrays.asList("2", "3", "4"));
grid.buildClassifier(trainingData);
```

Best Practices for Model Evaluation and Tuning

1. **Use Multiple Metrics**: Evaluate models using various metrics to gain a comprehensive understanding of performance.
2. **Cross-Validation**: Always use cross-validation to assess generalization and reduce variance in performance estimates.
3. **Document Experiments**: Keep track of hyperparameter settings, evaluation results, and insights gained during model development for future reference.
4. **Be Mindful of Overfitting**: Regularly monitor performance on both training and validation sets to detect overfitting early.
5. **Iterate and Experiment**: Model evaluation and tuning should be iterative processes. Don't hesitate to experiment with different approaches and configurations.

Conclusion

Model evaluation and hyperparameter tuning are vital to developing effective machine learning models. By understanding various evaluation metrics, validation techniques, and tuning strategies, practitioners can optimize model performance and ensure robust predictions. This knowledge will facilitate the effective use of Weka and other Java libraries in the machine learning workflow, leading to more successful data-driven solutions.

Chapter 13: Feature Selection and Engineering

Overview of Feature Selection and Engineering

Feature selection and engineering are critical processes in machine learning that significantly impact model performance. Effective selection and transformation of features can lead to improved accuracy, reduced complexity, and enhanced interpretability. This chapter delves into the importance of feature selection and engineering, explores various techniques, and provides practical guidance on their implementation using Java libraries like Weka.

Importance of Feature Selection and Engineering

1. **Improved Model Performance**: Selecting relevant features helps reduce noise and enhances the model's ability to learn patterns in the data.
2. **Reduced Overfitting**: By eliminating irrelevant or redundant features, models are less likely to memorize the training data, leading to better generalization on unseen data.
3. **Faster Training Time**: Fewer features lead to reduced computational complexity, allowing models to train faster and requiring less memory.
4. **Enhanced Interpretability**: A simpler model with fewer features is often easier to interpret, making it more understandable for stakeholders.

Feature Selection Techniques

Feature selection involves identifying and selecting a subset of relevant features for model training. Several techniques can be employed:

Filter Methods

Filter methods evaluate the relevance of features based on their intrinsic properties, independent of the learning algorithm. Common approaches include:

1. **Correlation Coefficient**: Measures the linear relationship between features and the target variable. High correlation values indicate strong relationships.
2. **Chi-Squared Test**: A statistical test that evaluates the independence of categorical features with respect to the target variable. Features with low p-values are considered more significant.

3. **Information Gain**: Measures the reduction in entropy (uncertainty) from knowing the value of a feature. Higher information gain indicates a more informative feature.
4. **Variance Threshold**: Removes features with low variance, assuming that low-variance features contribute little to the predictive power.

Wrapper Methods

Wrapper methods evaluate feature subsets based on their predictive power using a specific learning algorithm. This approach often leads to better performance but can be computationally expensive. Common techniques include:

1. **Forward Selection**: Starts with an empty set of features and adds one feature at a time based on the model's performance, selecting the feature that improves accuracy the most.
2. **Backward Elimination**: Begins with all features and removes one at a time, selecting the feature whose removal results in the least drop in model performance.
3. **Recursive Feature Elimination (RFE)**: A method that recursively removes the least important features based on model weights, focusing on the most relevant features.

Embedded Methods

Embedded methods perform feature selection during the model training process, combining the benefits of filter and wrapper methods. Examples include:

1. **Lasso Regression**: A linear regression method that includes an L1 penalty term, driving some feature coefficients to zero and effectively selecting features.
2. **Tree-based Methods**: Algorithms like Random Forests and Gradient Boosting provide feature importance scores based on the contribution of each feature to model performance, allowing for automatic feature selection.

Feature Engineering Techniques

Feature engineering involves transforming raw data into informative features that improve model performance. Key techniques include:

Transformation

1. **Normalization**: Scaling features to a common range, typically between 0 and 1, to improve model convergence and performance.
2. **Standardization**: Centering features by subtracting the mean and scaling by the standard deviation, often used in algorithms that assume normally distributed data.
3. **Log Transformation**: Applying a logarithmic transformation to skewed data to reduce the impact of extreme values.

Creation of New Features

1. **Polynomial Features**: Generating new features by taking combinations of existing features raised to a power. This can capture non-linear relationships.
2. **Interaction Features**: Creating new features by multiplying or combining existing features to capture interactions between them.
3. **Binning**: Converting continuous features into categorical bins, which can help capture non-linear relationships and reduce noise.
4. **Date and Time Features**: Extracting components such as year, month, day, or hour from date/time features to create new, relevant features.

Encoding Categorical Variables

1. **One-Hot Encoding**: Creating binary columns for each category of a categorical variable, allowing algorithms to process categorical features without ordinal assumptions.
2. **Label Encoding**: Assigning numerical labels to categories. This method is useful for ordinal variables but may introduce unwanted relationships for nominal variables.
3. **Target Encoding**: Replacing categorical values with the average of the target variable for each category, providing a numerical representation of categorical data.

Implementing Feature Selection and Engineering in Java

Using Weka for Feature Selection

Weka provides various tools for feature selection. For instance, you can easily implement filter methods using the `Remove` filter:

java
Copy code
```
// Load dataset
```

```java
Instances data = ...; // Load your data
// Filter for low-variance features
Remove remove = new Remove();
remove.setInputFormat(data);
remove.setAttributeIndices("1"); // Specify indices of features to remove
Instances filteredData = Filter.useFilter(data, remove);
```

For wrapper methods, you can use the `WrapperSubsetEval` class:

```java
// Use WrapperSubsetEval for feature selection
Classifier classifier = new J48();
WrapperSubsetEval eval = new WrapperSubsetEval();
eval.setClassifier(classifier);
eval.setEvaluationMetric(new Accuracy());
eval.buildEvaluator(data);
```

Feature Engineering with Weka

Weka's data preprocessing capabilities facilitate feature engineering. For instance, to apply normalization:

```java
// Normalize the dataset
Normalize normalize = new Normalize();
normalize.setInputFormat(data);
Instances normalizedData = Filter.useFilter(data, normalize);
```

To create new features, you may need to preprocess your data in Java before loading it into Weka, as it does not directly support complex transformations like polynomial features.

Example of Creating Interaction Features

You might need to manually create interaction features by iterating through the dataset:

java
Copy code
```
for (int i = 0; i < data.numInstances(); i++) {
        double   newFeature  =   data.instance(i).value(0)   *
data.instance(i).value(1); // Interaction of features 0 and 1
        data.instance(i).setValue(data.numAttributes()   -   1,
newFeature); // Set new feature at last position
}
```

Best Practices for Feature Selection and Engineering

1. **Understand Your Data**: Always start with a thorough exploratory data analysis (EDA) to understand the relationships and distributions of features.
2. **Iterative Process**: Feature selection and engineering should be iterative, refining features based on model performance and insights.
3. **Evaluate Feature Importance**: Use models that provide feature importance scores to identify and select relevant features systematically.
4. **Avoid Overengineering**: While creating new features can improve model performance, excessive complexity can lead to overfitting. Strive for a balance between complexity and interpretability.
5. **Document Transformations**: Maintain clear documentation of all feature selection and engineering processes to ensure reproducibility and transparency.

Conclusion

Feature selection and engineering are pivotal steps in the machine learning pipeline, significantly influencing model accuracy and efficiency. By employing various techniques for selecting and transforming features, practitioners can enhance their models' performance and interpretability. This foundational knowledge will support effective implementations using Java and Weka, ultimately leading to more successful data-driven solutions.

Chapter 14: Ensemble Learning Techniques

Overview of Ensemble Learning Techniques

Ensemble learning is a powerful approach in machine learning that combines multiple models to improve overall performance, robustness, and accuracy. By leveraging the strengths of various algorithms, ensemble methods can often outperform individual models. This chapter explores the fundamentals of ensemble learning, popular techniques, and their implementation using Java libraries, particularly Weka.

Importance of Ensemble Learning

1. **Improved Accuracy**: By aggregating predictions from multiple models, ensemble methods often yield better accuracy than single models, especially in complex datasets.
2. **Robustness**: Ensembles can reduce the impact of overfitting and variance, making models more reliable and generalizable to unseen data.
3. **Flexibility**: Ensemble methods can be applied to a wide range of algorithms and are not limited to any specific type of model, allowing for tailored solutions to various problems.
4. **Error Reduction**: Combining models helps to cancel out errors made by individual learners, leading to a more stable prediction.

Types of Ensemble Learning Methods

Ensemble learning methods can be broadly classified into two categories: bagging and boosting.

Bagging (Bootstrap Aggregating)

Bagging aims to reduce variance by training multiple models independently on different subsets of the data and averaging their predictions. The key steps include:

1. **Bootstrapping**: Randomly sampling the dataset with replacement to create multiple training subsets. Each subset may have duplicates, and some instances from the original dataset may not be included.
2. **Model Training**: A base model (often a decision tree) is trained on each bootstrap sample.

3. **Aggregation**: For regression tasks, the predictions of individual models are averaged. For classification tasks, the majority vote is taken as the final prediction.

Random Forest

One of the most popular bagging algorithms is Random Forest, which builds multiple decision trees and merges their results. It introduces additional randomness by selecting a subset of features for splitting at each node, enhancing diversity among the trees.

Key Features of Random Forest:

- **Feature Importance**: Provides insights into which features contribute most to predictions, helping with feature selection.
- **Overfitting Resistance**: By averaging many trees, Random Forest reduces the risk of overfitting compared to individual decision trees.

Boosting

Boosting focuses on converting weak learners (models that perform slightly better than random chance) into a strong learner by sequentially training models. Each new model attempts to correct errors made by the previous ones. The key steps include:

1. **Sequential Learning**: Models are trained in sequence, with each new model trained on the errors of the previous one.
2. **Weighted Voting**: Predictions from all models are combined, with more weight given to models that performed better on previous rounds.

AdaBoost

Adaptive Boosting (AdaBoost) is one of the earliest and most widely used boosting algorithms. It assigns weights to each training instance and adjusts them after each model is trained based on the errors made.

Key Features of AdaBoost:

- **Focus on Misclassified Instances**: Instances that are misclassified by the previous model receive higher weights, encouraging subsequent models to learn from their mistakes.
- **Sensitivity to Noisy Data**: While AdaBoost can improve performance, it may also amplify the impact of noise in the data, leading to overfitting.

Gradient Boosting

Gradient Boosting builds models sequentially while optimizing a loss function. It uses gradient descent to minimize the error of the ensemble by fitting each new model to the residuals of the previous models.

Key Features of Gradient Boosting:

- **Flexibility**: Can optimize any differentiable loss function, making it suitable for both regression and classification tasks.
- **Regularization**: Techniques like shrinkage and subsampling can help prevent overfitting.

Implementing Ensemble Learning in Java with Weka

Weka provides several built-in implementations of ensemble learning methods, making it easy to experiment with these techniques.

Using Random Forest in Weka

To implement a Random Forest model in Weka, you can use the following code snippet:

```java
Copy code
// Load dataset
Instances data = ...; // Load your dataset
data.setClassIndex(data.numAttributes() - 1); // Set the target attribute

// Build Random Forest model
RandomForest rf = new RandomForest();
rf.setNumTrees(100); // Set the number of trees
rf.buildClassifier(data);

// Evaluate model
Evaluation eval = new Evaluation(data);
eval.evaluateModel(rf, data);
System.out.println(eval.toSummaryString());
```

Using AdaBoost in Weka

To use AdaBoost, you can set it up as follows:

java
Copy code
```
// Load dataset
Instances data = ...; // Load your dataset
data.setClassIndex(data.numAttributes() - 1); // Set the target attribute

// Build AdaBoost model
AdaBoostM1 adaBoost = new AdaBoostM1();
adaBoost.setClassifier(new J48()); // Base classifier, e.g., a decision tree
adaBoost.buildClassifier(data);

// Evaluate model
Evaluation eval = new Evaluation(data);
eval.evaluateModel(adaBoost, data);
System.out.println(eval.toSummaryString());
```

Using Gradient Boosting in Weka

Weka supports Gradient Boosting through the `LogitBoost` classifier, which can be implemented as follows:

java
Copy code
```
// Load dataset
Instances data = ...; // Load your dataset
data.setClassIndex(data.numAttributes() - 1); // Set the target attribute

// Build Gradient Boosting model
LogitBoost logitBoost = new LogitBoost();
```

```
logitBoost.setNumIterations(100); // Set the number of boosting
iterations
logitBoost.buildClassifier(data);

// Evaluate model
Evaluation eval = new Evaluation(data);
eval.evaluateModel(logitBoost, data);
System.out.println(eval.toSummaryString());
```

Best Practices for Ensemble Learning

1. **Diversity is Key**: The effectiveness of ensemble methods often relies on the diversity of the individual models. Using different algorithms or varying model parameters can enhance diversity.
2. **Avoid Overfitting**: While ensembles can reduce overfitting, care must be taken, especially with boosting methods. Regularization techniques and cross-validation should be employed to ensure generalizability.
3. **Use Ensemble Stacking**: Stacking involves training multiple models and using their predictions as input for a final model. This can capture more complex relationships in the data.
4. **Monitor Performance**: Regularly evaluate the performance of the ensemble model on validation datasets to ensure it maintains its effectiveness as new data is introduced.
5. **Leverage Feature Importance**: Utilize the feature importance scores provided by models like Random Forest to guide feature selection and improve model efficiency.

Conclusion

Ensemble learning techniques provide powerful methods for improving model performance, robustness, and accuracy. By combining multiple models, practitioners can achieve superior results that often surpass those of individual models. Understanding and implementing these techniques using Java and Weka equips data scientists with essential tools for tackling complex machine learning problems effectively.

Chapter 15: Model Deployment and Maintenance

Overview of Model Deployment and Maintenance

Once a machine learning model has been trained and validated, the next critical step is deployment. Model deployment involves integrating the model into a production environment where it can make predictions on real-time data. However, deployment is just the beginning; ongoing maintenance is essential to ensure the model continues to perform well over time. This chapter covers the processes involved in deploying machine learning models, the challenges faced, and strategies for maintaining and updating models effectively.

Importance of Model Deployment

1. **Real-World Application**: Deployment allows the model to provide actionable insights and predictions in real-world scenarios, moving beyond theoretical performance metrics.
2. **Business Value**: Successfully deployed models can drive significant business value, enhancing decision-making processes, optimizing operations, and improving customer experiences.
3. **Feedback Loop**: Deployment creates a feedback loop where the model's predictions can be compared against actual outcomes, facilitating continuous improvement.

Steps in Model Deployment

Deploying a machine learning model involves several key steps:

1. Model Serialization

Before deploying, the trained model must be serialized or saved in a format that can be easily loaded and used in production. Common serialization formats include:

- **PMML (Predictive Model Markup Language)**: A standard format that allows models to be shared and reused across different systems.
- **Pickle**: A Python-specific format for serializing objects.
- **JSON or XML**: Lightweight data-interchange formats, suitable for simpler models or configurations.

In Weka, models can be serialized as follows:

```java
// Save the model to a file
ObjectOutputStream oos = new ObjectOutputStream(new FileOutputStream("model.dat"));
oos.writeObject(model);
oos.close();
```

2. Setting Up the Production Environment

The production environment must be configured to support the model. This includes:

- **Choosing the Right Platform**: Decide whether to deploy on-premises or in the cloud. Cloud platforms like AWS, Azure, and Google Cloud provide scalable resources and services tailored for machine learning.
- **Setting Up APIs**: Develop RESTful APIs to expose model predictions. This allows other applications to interact with the model seamlessly.
- **Containerization**: Using Docker or Kubernetes can help package the model and its dependencies, ensuring consistency across different environments.

3. Model Integration

Integrating the model into existing applications or workflows involves several considerations:

- **Data Input**: Ensure that the input data format aligns with the model's expectations. This may require data preprocessing or transformation steps.
- **Prediction Output**: Define how predictions will be returned to the user or application, including formatting and any necessary post-processing.
- **Monitoring**: Implement monitoring systems to track the model's performance in real time. Key metrics to monitor include latency, accuracy, and resource utilization.

4. Testing in Production

Before fully launching the model, conduct testing in the production environment:

- **Shadow Testing**: Run the model in parallel with existing systems without affecting the output. This allows for performance comparisons and validation against live data.
- **A/B Testing**: Deploy the model to a subset of users while the previous version continues to operate for others. Compare performance metrics to assess the new model's effectiveness.

Challenges in Model Deployment

Deploying machine learning models can present several challenges:

1. Data Drift

Data drift occurs when the statistical properties of the input data change over time, which can lead to model performance degradation. This may result from changes in user behavior, market conditions, or other external factors.

2. Model Versioning

Keeping track of different model versions can be complex, especially when multiple models are being developed simultaneously. Implementing a version control system helps manage model iterations and ensures that the correct model is deployed.

3. Scalability

As the volume of data and the number of predictions increase, the deployment environment must be capable of scaling efficiently to handle the load. This may involve optimizing infrastructure, load balancing, or utilizing cloud-based solutions.

4. Security Concerns

Ensuring that the deployed model and the data it processes are secure is critical. This includes safeguarding against unauthorized access, data leaks, and ensuring compliance with regulations such as GDPR.

Model Maintenance Strategies

Ongoing maintenance is essential to ensure that deployed models remain effective over time. Key strategies include:

1. Regular Monitoring and Evaluation

Continuous monitoring of model performance helps identify issues early. Key practices include:

- **Performance Metrics**: Regularly track accuracy, precision, recall, and other relevant metrics to assess model performance against baseline expectations.
- **User Feedback**: Collect feedback from users to understand how the model's predictions are being received and to identify any shortcomings.

2. Periodic Retraining

Retraining models periodically helps maintain their relevance as data distributions change. This involves:

- **Data Collection**: Continuously gather new data and update the training dataset.
- **Model Update Schedule**: Establish a schedule for retraining the model based on performance metrics or data drift indicators.

3. Automated Monitoring Systems

Implement automated systems to detect performance drops or data drift, triggering alerts for further investigation. These systems can also initiate retraining processes automatically.

4. Model Explainability

Ensuring that the model remains interpretable over time is essential for trust and compliance. Use tools and techniques that provide insights into model decisions and performance, especially as the model evolves.

Best Practices for Model Deployment and Maintenance

1. **Establish Clear KPIs**: Define clear key performance indicators (KPIs) for success, including accuracy, latency, and user satisfaction.
2. **Implement Version Control**: Use version control systems not only for the model but also for the code and data used in deployment.
3. **Automate Where Possible**: Automate as much of the deployment and maintenance process as possible to reduce human error and streamline operations.
4. **Document Everything**: Maintain thorough documentation for all deployment processes, model versions, and maintenance activities to ensure transparency and reproducibility.

5. **Engage Stakeholders**: Involve stakeholders throughout the deployment process to ensure that the model meets business needs and aligns with organizational goals.

Conclusion

Model deployment and maintenance are crucial stages in the machine learning lifecycle that determine the long-term success of machine learning initiatives. By following best practices and addressing challenges proactively, organizations can effectively integrate models into production environments, ensuring that they continue to deliver value over time. Understanding the nuances of deployment and maintenance empowers data scientists and engineers to create robust, scalable solutions that adapt to changing conditions and user needs.

Chapter 16: Ethical Considerations in Machine Learning

Overview of Ethical Considerations in Machine Learning

As machine learning technologies become increasingly pervasive, ethical considerations surrounding their development and deployment are gaining prominence. These considerations encompass a wide range of issues, including fairness, accountability, transparency, and privacy. This chapter explores the ethical challenges inherent in machine learning, examines frameworks for ethical decision-making, and provides strategies for implementing ethical practices in machine learning projects.

Importance of Ethical Considerations

1. **Public Trust**: Addressing ethical concerns helps build trust between organizations and the public, ensuring that machine learning systems are perceived as responsible and reliable.
2. **Social Responsibility**: Developers and organizations have a social responsibility to mitigate potential harms caused by their models, including bias and discrimination.
3. **Compliance and Regulation**: Increasing regulatory scrutiny demands that organizations adhere to ethical guidelines and legal standards in their machine learning practices.
4. **Sustainable Development**: Ethical considerations contribute to the sustainability of machine learning technologies, ensuring they are used to promote positive societal outcomes.

Key Ethical Issues in Machine Learning

1. Bias and Fairness

Bias in machine learning can lead to unfair treatment of individuals or groups based on attributes such as race, gender, or socioeconomic status. Sources of bias may include:

- **Data Bias**: Training datasets may reflect historical biases, leading models to perpetuate these biases in their predictions.
- **Algorithmic Bias**: Certain algorithms may favor specific outcomes over others, exacerbating existing inequalities.

Fairness Metrics: Various metrics exist to evaluate fairness, such as demographic parity, equal opportunity, and disparate impact. Organizations should choose appropriate metrics based on the context of their application.

2. Transparency and Explainability

Transparency involves providing insights into how machine learning models make decisions. Explainability is crucial for several reasons:

- **User Trust**: Users are more likely to trust systems that provide clear explanations for their predictions.
- **Regulatory Compliance**: Some regulations require organizations to explain automated decisions, particularly in sensitive domains like finance and healthcare.

Methods for improving explainability include:

- **Interpretable Models**: Opting for simpler, more interpretable models when possible.
- **Post-Hoc Explanations**: Utilizing tools like LIME or SHAP to provide explanations for predictions made by complex models.

3. Privacy and Data Protection

Machine learning often relies on vast amounts of data, raising concerns about privacy and data protection:

- **Personal Data**: The use of personal data without proper consent can violate privacy rights and regulations such as GDPR.
- **Anonymization**: Techniques to anonymize data may not always be effective, leading to the potential re-identification of individuals.

Organizations should prioritize data minimization, ensuring only necessary data is collected, and implement robust data protection measures.

4. Accountability and Responsibility

Establishing accountability for machine learning systems is crucial for ethical deployment:

- **Responsibility**: Organizations must clarify who is responsible for the outcomes produced by machine learning models, particularly in high-stakes scenarios.

- **Auditability**: Maintaining records of model development, training data, and decision-making processes can enhance accountability and enable audits.

5. Societal Impact

Machine learning can have far-reaching societal impacts, both positive and negative. Ethical considerations should encompass:

- **Potential Harms**: Assessing the potential for harm to individuals or communities as a result of model deployment.
- **Beneficial Use**: Ensuring that machine learning technologies are used to promote social good and address pressing societal issues.

Frameworks for Ethical Decision-Making

Several frameworks can guide ethical decision-making in machine learning:

1. The Fairness Framework

This framework emphasizes the importance of fairness in model development and deployment. Key components include:

- **Identify Biases**: Systematically identify and analyze potential biases in data and algorithms.
- **Evaluate Impact**: Assess the impact of model decisions on different demographic groups.
- **Mitigation Strategies**: Implement strategies to mitigate identified biases and ensure fair outcomes.

2. The Accountability Framework

The accountability framework focuses on establishing clear lines of responsibility for machine learning systems. Key steps include:

- **Define Roles**: Clearly define roles and responsibilities for individuals involved in model development and deployment.
- **Create Documentation**: Maintain thorough documentation of decision-making processes, data sources, and model evaluations.

3. The Transparency Framework

This framework advocates for transparency in machine learning practices:

- **Explainability**: Develop mechanisms to provide clear explanations for model predictions.
- **Open Communication**: Foster open communication with stakeholders about model limitations, data usage, and potential biases.

4. The Ethical Review Framework

Organizations can establish ethical review boards to evaluate machine learning projects:

- **Interdisciplinary Review**: Include diverse perspectives in the review process, ensuring consideration of ethical implications from various angles.
- **Stakeholder Engagement**: Engage with affected communities and stakeholders to gather input on potential ethical concerns.

Strategies for Implementing Ethical Practices

To implement ethical practices in machine learning projects, organizations can take several proactive steps:

1. Conduct Ethical Assessments

Before deploying a model, conduct ethical assessments to evaluate potential risks and impacts. This should include a review of data sources, model performance, and potential biases.

2. Promote Diversity in Teams

Diverse teams can provide varied perspectives on ethical issues, reducing the likelihood of blind spots. Organizations should prioritize diversity in hiring and project teams.

3. Invest in Education and Training

Providing training on ethical considerations for data scientists and stakeholders can enhance awareness and foster a culture of responsibility. Topics may include bias detection, transparency, and privacy.

4. Engage with the Community

Involve external stakeholders, including community organizations and advocacy groups, to gather feedback and ensure that diverse voices are considered in decision-making.

5. Establish Ethical Guidelines

Develop and implement ethical guidelines that govern machine learning practices within the organization. These guidelines should be regularly reviewed and updated to reflect evolving societal norms and regulations.

Conclusion

Ethical considerations are paramount in the development and deployment of machine learning systems. By addressing issues of bias, transparency, privacy, accountability, and societal impact, organizations can ensure that their models are not only effective but also responsible and aligned with societal values. Implementing ethical frameworks and practices will enhance public trust, promote social responsibility, and contribute to the sustainable development of machine learning technologies. As the field continues to evolve, ongoing dialogue and reflection on ethical practices will be essential for fostering innovation that benefits society as a whole.

Chapter 17: Future Trends in Machine Learning

Overview of Future Trends in Machine Learning

The field of machine learning is rapidly evolving, driven by advances in technology, an increasing volume of data, and a growing understanding of complex algorithms. This chapter explores the emerging trends that are shaping the future of machine learning, focusing on innovations in algorithms, applications, and ethical considerations. Understanding these trends can provide insights into how organizations can prepare for the changing landscape of machine learning.

Importance of Staying Ahead of Trends

1. **Competitive Advantage**: Organizations that stay informed about emerging trends can leverage new technologies to gain a competitive edge.
2. **Innovation**: Being aware of future directions can inspire innovative solutions and new applications of machine learning.
3. **Adaptability**: Understanding trends allows organizations to adapt their strategies and operations in response to technological advancements.
4. **Preparation for Challenges**: Anticipating changes in the landscape can help organizations prepare for potential challenges, such as ethical dilemmas or regulatory shifts.

Emerging Trends in Machine Learning

1. Automated Machine Learning (AutoML)

AutoML refers to the process of automating the end-to-end process of applying machine learning to real-world problems. Key features of AutoML include:

- **Model Selection**: Automatically selecting the best model for a given dataset based on performance metrics.
- **Hyperparameter Optimization**: Streamlining the process of tuning model parameters to improve accuracy.
- **Feature Engineering**: Automating the extraction and selection of relevant features from raw data.

Impact of AutoML: AutoML democratizes machine learning, making it accessible to non-experts and allowing data scientists to focus on higher-level tasks.

2. Explainable AI (XAI)

As machine learning models become more complex, the need for transparency and interpretability is growing. Explainable AI aims to provide insights into how models make decisions. Key components include:

- **Model Interpretability**: Developing methods that allow users to understand the reasoning behind model predictions.
- **Regulatory Compliance**: Ensuring models comply with regulations that require explanations for automated decisions, particularly in sensitive domains.

Importance of XAI: Explainable AI fosters trust among users and stakeholders, enabling responsible deployment of machine learning systems.

3. Federated Learning

Federated learning is an approach that allows multiple devices to collaboratively train a model while keeping data localized. Key benefits include:

- **Privacy Preservation**: Reducing the need to transfer sensitive data to central servers, thereby enhancing privacy.
- **Reduced Latency**: Training models closer to data sources can improve response times and reduce bandwidth usage.

Future of Federated Learning: As privacy regulations become stricter, federated learning may become increasingly important in applications such as healthcare and finance.

4. Ethical AI and Governance

The growing awareness of ethical considerations in AI is driving the development of frameworks for ethical AI and governance. Key trends include:

- **Standardization**: Efforts to create standardized guidelines and best practices for ethical AI development and deployment.
- **Accountability Mechanisms**: Establishing frameworks to hold organizations accountable for the impacts of their AI systems.

Impact of Ethical AI: Ethical considerations will increasingly influence decision-making processes in organizations, shaping public perception and regulatory compliance.

5. Integration of AI and IoT

The convergence of artificial intelligence (AI) and the Internet of Things (IoT) is enabling smarter and more responsive systems. Key applications include:

- **Smart Cities**: Utilizing AI to analyze data from IoT devices for traffic management, resource allocation, and public safety.
- **Predictive Maintenance**: Using AI to predict equipment failures in industrial settings, improving operational efficiency.

Future Implications: As IoT devices proliferate, the integration of AI will enhance decision-making capabilities across various sectors.

6. Edge Computing and On-Device Learning

Edge computing involves processing data closer to its source rather than relying on centralized cloud resources. Key benefits include:

- **Reduced Latency**: Minimizing the time it takes to process and respond to data inputs, crucial for real-time applications.
- **Bandwidth Efficiency**: Reducing the amount of data transmitted to cloud servers, lowering costs and improving efficiency.

Role of On-Device Learning: Machine learning models that operate directly on devices (e.g., smartphones, sensors) will become more prevalent, allowing for personalized experiences and greater privacy.

7. Enhanced Natural Language Processing (NLP)

Advancements in natural language processing are paving the way for more sophisticated interactions between humans and machines. Key developments include:

- **Contextual Understanding**: Models that better understand context and nuances in human language, improving the accuracy of text analysis and conversational agents.
- **Multimodal Learning**: Combining text, audio, and visual inputs to create richer interactions and more robust applications.

Impact on Applications: Enhanced NLP will lead to more effective chatbots, virtual assistants, and language translation services.

8. Advanced Reinforcement Learning

Reinforcement learning (RL) continues to evolve, with applications in areas such as robotics, gaming, and autonomous systems. Key advancements include:

- **Hierarchical Reinforcement Learning**: Developing more sophisticated RL architectures that can learn complex tasks by breaking them down into simpler sub-tasks.
- **Transfer Learning in RL**: Leveraging knowledge gained in one environment to improve performance in another, accelerating the learning process.

Future Applications: Advanced RL techniques will drive innovations in automation, personalization, and strategic decision-making.

Conclusion

The future of machine learning is poised for significant advancements, with trends such as AutoML, explainable AI, federated learning, and ethical governance shaping the landscape. Organizations that stay informed and adaptable to these emerging trends will be better positioned to leverage the full potential of machine learning technologies, driving innovation and responsible use in various applications. Embracing these trends will not only enhance operational efficiency but also contribute to the broader goal of creating equitable and beneficial AI systems for society. As the field continues to evolve, ongoing dialogue and research will be essential to navigate the challenges and opportunities that lie ahead.

www.ingramcontent.com/pod-product-compliance
Lightning Source LLC
Chambersburg PA
CBHW062114220526
45471CB00010B/3738